Fractions, Decimals and Percentages

Fractions 2

Teacher's Guide

Hilary Koll and Steve Mills

Schofield&Sims

Free downloads available from the Schofield & Sims website

A selection of free downloads is available from the Schofield & Sims website (www.schofieldandsims.co.uk/free-downloads). These may be used to further enhance the effectiveness of the programme. The downloads add to the range of print materials supplied in the teacher's guides.

- **Graphics** slides containing the visual elements from each teacher's guide unit provided as Microsoft PowerPoint® presentations.

- **Go deeper investigations** providing additional extension material to develop problem-solving and reasoning skills.

- **Additional resources** including a fraction wall, a comparison chart and number lines to support learning and teaching.

Published by **Schofield & Sims Ltd**, Dogley Mill, Fenay Bridge, Huddersfield HD8 0NQ, UK
Telephone 01484 607080
www.schofieldandsims.co.uk

This edition copyright © Schofield & Sims Ltd, 2017
First published in 2017

Authors: **Hilary Koll and Steve Mills**
Hilary Koll and Steve Mills have asserted their moral rights under the Copyright, Designs and Patents Act, 1988, to be identified as the authors of this work.

British Library Cataloguing in Publication Data
A catalogue record for this book is available from the British Library.

Design by **Oxford Designers & Illustrators Ltd**
Printed in the UK by **Page Bros (Norwich) Ltd**

ISBN 978 07217 1378 6

Contents

Overview

Fractions, decimals and percentages are frequent areas of difficulty in mathematics for primary school pupils. Many teachers find them challenging to teach and pupils often have limited or only partially developed conceptual understanding of the topics. A major reason children struggle with fractions, decimals and percentages is the variety of contexts and representations in which they appear – for example, as areas, as sets, on number lines, as a result of a division problem and in relation to measurements.

Schofield & Sims Fractions, Decimals and Percentages is a structured whole-school programme designed to help pupils develop a deep, secure and adaptable understanding of these topics. The series consists of six pupil books and six teacher's guides, one for each primary school year.

Each unit of the programme addresses a single learning objective. The teacher's guides provide detailed teaching notes with accompanying graphics to use in lessons. The pupil books provide a summary of the learning objective and a set of related practice questions that increase in difficulty. This allows you, the teacher or adult helper, to introduce and teach a particular concept and then to provide appropriate intelligent practice which gradually leads children towards more complex representations and varied contexts.

Supporting a mastery approach, all pupils are encouraged to move at the same pace through the units and are given the same opportunity to fully understand the concept being taught. Depth of learning is emphasised over speed of learning and the pupils should have a solid understanding of the content of each unit before moving on to new material. Downloadable **Go deeper** extension resources help to cement pupils' understanding of the concepts that have been taught. The series also provides ongoing and integrated assessment throughout.

Fractions 2 and the National Curriculum

Fractions 2 and its related **Teacher's Guide** match the statutory requirements for Year 2 for 'Fractions' in the National Curriculum. The two statutory requirements are listed below. They have been coded for ease of reference. For example, Y2/F1 refers to the first fractions requirement in Year 2.

National Curriculum requirements for 'Fractions'

Y2/F1 Recognise, find, name and write fractions $\frac{1}{3}$, $\frac{1}{4}$, $\frac{2}{4}$ and $\frac{3}{4}$ of a length, shape, set of objects or quantity.

Y2/F2 Write simple fractions, for example $\frac{1}{2}$ of 6 = 3, and recognise the equivalence of $\frac{2}{4}$ and $\frac{1}{2}$.

The series sets quite demanding expectations for reading ability which some children may find challenging. To ensure that the children are all given the opportunity to succeed, it is helpful, where possible, for an adult to work through the materials with groups and to read each question aloud. This may also encourage good discussion between the children and can help you to spot and challenge misconceptions.

National Curriculum coverage chart

This chart maps all the units and tests in **Fractions 2** against the National Curriculum requirements. When reading the chart, please refer to the curriculum coding introduced on page 4. The light shaded boxes show where a requirement is touched upon and the dark shaded boxes show the key units and tests for that requirement.

	Y1 Revision	Y2/F1	Y2/F2
Unit 1	■	■	
Unit 2	■	■	
Unit 3		▨	▨
Unit 4			■
Unit 5		■	■
Unit 6			■
Check-up test 1		■	■
Unit 7		■	■
Unit 8		■	
Unit 9		■	
Unit 10		■	■
Unit 11		▨	■
Unit 12		■	
Check-up test 2		■	■
Final test		■	■

Prerequisites for Fractions 2

Before beginning **Fractions 2** the children should have a basic understanding of halves and quarters. Each year of the programme, however, begins with revision to ensure that the children understand the necessary ideas to move forward. The first column in the National Curriculum coverage chart on page 5, labelled 'Y1 Revision', shows the units that revise Year 1 material. The children can be given **Fractions 1** first if they require further practice to build their confidence and understanding.

The focus in Year 2 is on the following areas: one-third, one-quarter, two-quarters and three-quarters and the notation for each, writing simple fractions, recognising the equivalence of two-quarters and one-half, and problem solving.

Fractions 2 Teacher's Guide

The **Fractions 2 Teacher's Guide** contains everything you need to teach the National Curriculum requirements for 'Fractions' in Year 2. There are 12 corresponding units in the teacher's guide and pupil book, four for each term.

Using the Teacher's notes

In this teacher's guide you will find **Teacher's notes** for each unit (pages 12 to 35). These include a detailed lesson plan with accompanying graphics that can be used to demonstrate the learning objective before the children begin the activities in the pupil book. The graphics are visual prompts for the class and can be used in a variety of ways. They are all available as interactive PowerPoint® presentations (free to download from the Schofield & Sims website). Alternatively, the graphics could be presented on a projector, or photocopied and used as pupil handouts, or used as a guide when drawing your own visual prompts. The lesson plans can be easily adapted to suit your classroom. Below is an example lesson from this teacher's guide, alongside the corresponding slides from the **Fractions 2** Powerpoint® presentation.

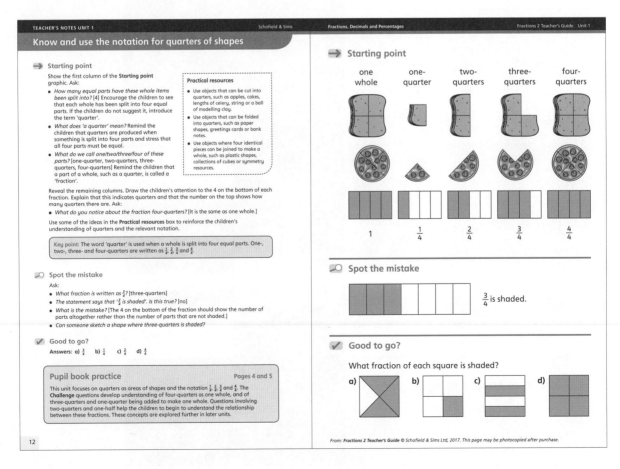

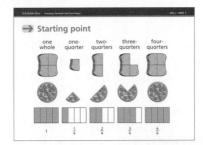 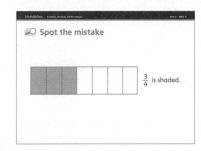

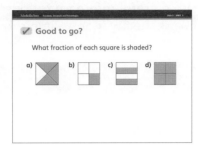

The **Teacher's notes** for each unit are divided into the following sections:

- **Starting point** – This section provides clear instruction on how to introduce and teach the learning objective. Using the graphics as prompts, probing questions are given that draw on the children's prior knowledge and encourage them to find connections, reason and reach conclusions about why the concept being taught is true. The **Key point** of the lesson is clearly highlighted.

- **Practical resources** – This box provides suggestions for practical resources and materials that you can use with the children to develop each idea. Some children may initially struggle with the concept of fractions and so they should be given plenty of opportunities for concepts to be embedded through demonstration and practice with real objects. There are also links to the photocopiable resources that can be found at the back of this book. These include cards and posters that can be used in conjunction with real-life materials, for example, in identifying whether or not objects are correctly split in half. These resources can be cut out and laminated for more permanent classroom use or used as displays to stimulate discussion.

- **Spot the mistake** – This is a statement, often with a visual element, that represents a mistake which is commonly made with the concept being taught. The statement is intentionally incorrect. You are given a series of corrective questions to ask the children, drawing out potential misconceptions and helping them to spot the mistake. Procedural understanding is deepened as the children discuss why the statement is incorrect and what the correct statement should be.

- **Good to go?** – This section has quick practice questions that help you establish whether each child has understood the lesson and is a useful tool for formative assessment. It is suggested that the children answer these questions on mini-whiteboards and hold up their answers. This helps you to quickly identify the children who require further assistance and those who have fully understood the unit focus.

- **Pupil book practice** – This section provides links to the pupil book pages for this unit. It flags potential areas of difficulty to be aware of in the activities, highlights when questions act as a bridge to later units, and offers further suggestions for practical resources you can use to support the children as they work.

Answers

The teacher's guide contains a complete set of **Answers** (pages 36 to 65) for all the units and tests in the pupil book. The answers are presented as correctly completed pupil book pages to make marking quick and easy.

Fractions 2 Pupil Book

Once you are confident that the children have grasped the concept of the lesson, they should turn to the corresponding unit in their pupil book. This offers varied activities of increasing difficulty that provide plenty of repetition, practice and challenge to consolidate learning.

The pupil book begins with a simple introduction which clearly explains the purpose of the book and how it is used. This introduction supports your own instructions for the children as they start this book. It is also a useful reference for parents if you decide to set sections of the pupil book as homework. Below is an example lesson from the pupil book.

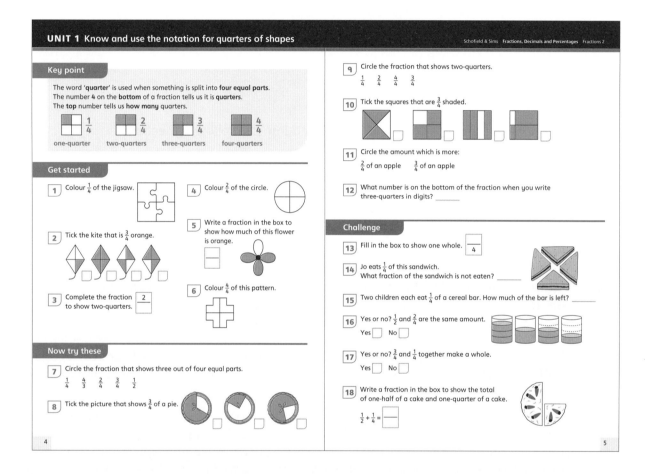

Each unit in the pupil book begins with a child-friendly summary of the **Key point** of the lesson, as a reminder for the child and to assist parents in supporting their children at home.

The practice questions in each unit are divided into three sections.

- **Get started** – Quick questions to help the child gain confidence in the topic, with a variety of straightforward practice questions related to the learning objective.

- **Now try these** – Additional number and practical problems to take the topic further with more varied vocabulary and representations.

- **Challenge** – Problem-solving questions involving greater challenge, such as measurement and money contexts and links to other more complex concepts.

The children should write their answers directly into their own pupil book. Each completed pupil book provides a permanent record of achievement and encourages the children to take pride in their work. Two **Check-up tests**, a **Final test** and a **How did I find it?** checklist are also included in each pupil book. These help you to monitor the children's progress.

Strategies for learning

If a child is struggling with a question, prompt them to try it again using a different strategy. Problem-solving strategies develop deeper mathematical thinking, allowing children to solve a wider variety of problems.

- **Visualising** – *Can you draw a picture or use some practical equipment to help you?*

- **Simplifying** – *If a problem seems too difficult, make it easier. What if the question was asking about halves rather than quarters. Could you do it then?*

- **Reasoning** – *Talking to someone about a tricky problem can be helpful. Ask your partner to explain it to you or explain it to them, if you can.*

- **Looking for patterns** – *Look out for patterns in the numbers in a problem. Sometimes you can find an answer more quickly by spotting a pattern and continuing it.*

- **Checking** – *Go back and check your answers or work with a friend to check each other's.*

- **Persevering** – *When all else fails, keep going! You could use a coloured pencil to highlight the important numbers in the problem. See if that helps you to spot a pattern.*

Go deeper

When teaching for mastery, differentiation is achieved by emphasising depth of knowledge and mathematical fluency over pace of learning. The **Challenge** questions in the pupil book offer sophisticated problems that will stretch even the more able child and provide the practice that is required to exceed the expected national standards. **Go deeper investigations** are also available (free to download from the Schofield & Sims website), which correspond with the content covered up to each **Check-up test**. These group work problem-solving activities help children to delve even more deeply into the concepts being taught and cement their understanding. Teacher's notes and pupil work sheets are provided for each investigation. These can be used with the whole class in a dedicated problem-solving lesson or as extension material for children who require further challenge.

Assessment

Fractions 2 and its related **Teacher's Guide** offer frequent opportunities and multiple resources for in-school assessment. These resources should be used in line with your school's own assessment policy.

Formative assessment

The teacher's guide lesson plans all feature precise questioning. This can be used as part of your ongoing formative assessment to test the children's conceptual and procedural knowledge. The questions can help to uncover a child's reasoning and depth of mathematical thinking. The **Good to go?** section at the end of each lesson provides a further check, enabling you to easily identify when children are struggling and when they are ready to progress to the pupil book practice questions.

The pupil book units can also be used as a basis for formative assessment. Teachers should monitor the progress that each child is making as they work through the pupil book questions. If an answer is incorrect, asking the child to explain how they reached this answer may reveal gaps in understanding that can then be addressed.

Two **Check-up tests** are provided in the pupil book. These can be used to test children's understanding of the material covered in the preceding six units. This allows you to ascertain how well the children have remembered the ideas covered in the programme so far and how secure their understanding is.

Each child's day-to-day progress can be monitored by using the **Pupil progress chart** (at the back of this book). This chart can be photocopied for each child in your class so that you can keep track of the marks scored on each unit and **Check-up test**. Guidance is provided below on how to interpret the information gained from the **Pupil progress chart**.

Decoding the unit scores

While the total score achieved in each pupil book unit will be a good indicator of the children's overall progress, it is advisable to keep an eye out for patterns in their scores across the three different sections as well.

- If a child struggles with **Get started**, it can indicate that the child has not yet understood or has misunderstood the concept of the unit and is likely to require further support.

- If a child struggles with **Now try these** after a successful **Get started**, it can indicate that the child has understood the initial idea but is having trouble applying it to different contexts and with different representations.

- If a child struggles with **Challenge** after a successful **Get started** and **Now try these**, it can indicate that the child may need further help in problem-solving processes such as reasoning, simplifying, visualising, looking for patterns or generalising. It may also indicate that the child is having difficulty with comprehension skills, misunderstanding the language that is used in the question.

- If the child is able to make a good attempt at **Challenge** after a successful **Get started** and **Now try these**, it can indicate that the child has mastered the unit and is secure in their understanding of the concepts that have been taught.

- If the child scores highly across all three sections, it can indicate that the child has mastered the concepts of the unit at greater depth.

- Look out for inconsistent scoring across the sections, for example, a low score in **Get started** and a high score in **Now try these** or a low score in **Now try these** and a high score in **Challenge** as this may mean that there are gaps in the child's understanding. Some guesswork may have been involved in gaining correct answers.

Decoding the Check-up test scores

- A score of 0–13 can indicate that the child has not yet understood all of the key concepts in the preceding units. Further consolidation work or a different approach may be needed to ensure secure understanding.

- A score of 14–18 can indicate that the child has mastered the concepts of the preceding units and can confidently move forward.

Each pupil book also contains a **How did I find it?** checklist which enables children to evaluate their own progress as they work through the programme. Each unit has a corresponding 'I can' statement. After completing each unit, **Check-up test** and **Final test** the children should be given the opportunity to rate how they found the unit – 'difficult', 'getting there' or 'easy'.

Summative assessment

The **Final test** in the pupil book can be used for in-school summative assessment at the end of **Fractions 2**. This test allows you to assess the children's understanding of all the concepts covered in **Fractions 2**. The **Final test** is organised so that each section tests a different statutory requirement for the Year 2 National Curriculum.

Marks for the **Final test** can be recorded on the **Final test group record sheet** (at the back of this book). Record each mark by either ticking or shading the relevant boxes next to each child's name. This chart outlines which curriculum requirement is being tested in each section using the curriculum coding that was introduced on page 4. It provides an at-a-glance overview of how the whole class is performing in relation to the National Curriculum requirements and enables you to evaluate pupil learning at the end of the year. Guidance is provided below on how to interpret the information gained from this chart.

Decoding the Final test scores

- A score of 0–14 marks can indicate that the child has not fully mastered the key concepts for the year. The curriculum coding should provide a clear idea of which requirements the child is struggling with. Catch-up work is likely to be needed in these areas before the child is ready to proceed with Year 3 material.

- A score of 15–20 marks can indicate that the child has mastered the key concepts for the year and can confidently move forward to Year 3 material. The curriculum coding should provide a clear idea of the child's strengths and warn of any areas of weakness that may require additional practice in Year 3.

The **Final test group record sheet** provides a useful record for school leaders and inspectors and will show the subsequent teacher how secure each child was in their knowledge of the previous year's curriculum and how ready they are for progression.

Know and use the notation for quarters of shapes

➡ Starting point

Show the first column of the **Starting point** graphic. Ask:

- *How many equal parts have these whole items been split into?* [4] Encourage the children to see that each whole has been split into four equal parts. If the children do not suggest it, introduce the term 'quarter'.

- *What does 'a quarter' mean?* Remind the children that quarters are produced when something is split into four parts and stress that all four parts must be equal.

- *What do we call one/two/three/four of these parts?* [one-quarter, two-quarters, three-quarters, four-quarters] Remind the children that a part of a whole, such as a quarter, is called a 'fraction'.

> **Practical resources**
>
> - Use objects that can be cut into quarters, such as apples, cakes, lengths of celery, string or a ball of modelling clay.
>
> - Use objects that can be folded into quarters, such as paper shapes, greetings cards or bank notes.
>
> - Use objects where four identical pieces can be joined to make a whole, such as plastic shapes, collections of cubes or symmetry resources.

Reveal the remaining columns. Draw the children's attention to the 4 on the bottom of each fraction. Explain that this indicates quarters and that the number on the top shows how many quarters there are. Ask:

- *What do you notice about the fraction four-quarters?* [It is the same as one whole.]

Use some of the ideas in the **Practical resources** box to reinforce the children's understanding of quarters and the relevant notation.

> **Key point:** The word 'quarter' is used when a whole is split into four equal parts. One-, two-, three- and four-quarters are written as $\frac{1}{4}$, $\frac{2}{4}$, $\frac{3}{4}$ and $\frac{4}{4}$.

Spot the mistake

Ask:

- *What fraction is written as $\frac{3}{4}$?* [three-quarters]
- *The statement says that '$\frac{3}{4}$ is shaded'. Is this true?* [no]
- *What is the mistake?* [The 4 on the bottom of the fraction should show the number of parts altogether rather than the number of parts that are not shaded.]
- *Can someone sketch a shape where three-quarters is shaded?*

✔ Good to go?

Answers: a) $\frac{3}{4}$ **b)** $\frac{1}{4}$ **c)** $\frac{2}{4}$ **d)** $\frac{4}{4}$

> ## Pupil book practice   Pages 4 and 5
>
> This unit focuses on quarters as areas of shapes and the notation $\frac{1}{4}$, $\frac{2}{4}$, $\frac{3}{4}$ and $\frac{4}{4}$. The **Challenge** questions develop understanding of four-quarters as one whole, and of three-quarters and one-quarter being added to make one whole. Questions involving two-quarters and one-half help the children to begin to understand the relationship between these fractions. These concepts are explored further in later units.

Starting point

one whole	one-quarter	two-quarters	three-quarters	four-quarters
				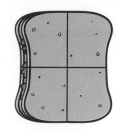
			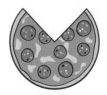	
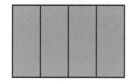	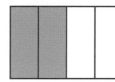	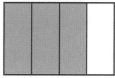		
1	$\frac{1}{4}$	$\frac{2}{4}$	$\frac{3}{4}$	$\frac{4}{4}$

 Spot the mistake

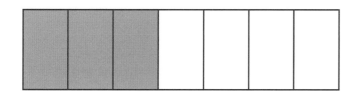 $\frac{3}{4}$ is shaded.

 Good to go?

What fraction of each square is shaded?

a) 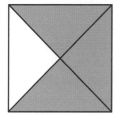   b) 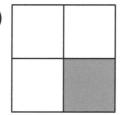   c) 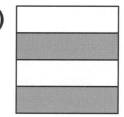   d)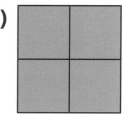

Know and use the notation for quarters of sets

➡ Starting point

Show graphic **A** without the text beneath. Ask:

- *How many equal groups have the t-shirts been arranged into?* [4]
- *When a whole set is split into four equal parts, what is each part called?* [a quarter]
- *How many quarters of the set are shaded?* [one-quarter]
- *How do we write one-quarter as a fraction?* [$\frac{1}{4}$]
- *How many groups are unshaded?* [3]
- *What fraction of the whole set is unshaded?* [three-quarters]
- *How do we write three-quarters as a fraction?* [$\frac{3}{4}$] Reveal the fractions.

Repeat the activity for graphic **B**, discussing the fraction of cubes that are shaded/unshaded first and then revealing the notation $\frac{2}{4}$.

Use some of the ideas in the **Practical resources** box to reinforce the children's understanding of quarters and the related notation.

Practical resources

- Linking cubes can help children to make the connection between quarters as areas of shapes and as sets of objects. For example, the sets in the **Starting point** graphics could be shown with orange and white cubes. Show the cubes individually and then join them to make sticks of cubes.

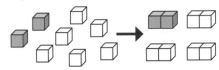

- The 'Quarters cards' and 'Quarters of sets cards' at the back of the book can be used for matching activities. They include words, such as 'two-quarters', and notation, including '$\frac{2}{4}$'. The cards could be matched to sets of real objects.

> **Key point:** A whole set is split into four equal parts to make four quarters. One-, two-, three- and four-quarters are written as $\frac{1}{4}$, $\frac{2}{4}$, $\frac{3}{4}$ and $\frac{4}{4}$.

🔍 Spot the mistake

Ask:

- *The statement says '$\frac{1}{3}$ of the cubes are shaded'. Is this true?* [no]
- *What fraction of the cubes are actually shaded?* [$\frac{3}{4}$] Explain that there are 4 cubes altogether, so this is the number on the bottom of the fraction. 3 cubes are shaded so this is the number on the top of the fraction.

✔ Good to go?

Answers: a) $\frac{1}{4}$ **b)** $\frac{2}{4}$ or $\frac{1}{2}$ **c)** $\frac{3}{4}$

Pupil book practice    Pages 6 and 7

Provide the children with cubes or counters to help them with this work. If they are unsure, they could select a cube or counter to represent each item in the question and then sort them into four equal groups to find one-quarter. Observe which children can answer the **Challenge** questions without using equipment or visual representations. For example, some children will be able to visualise three-quarters of 8 grapes in their heads for question 14, or use information from previous answers to answer a subsequent question.

 **Starting point**

A

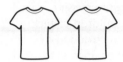　　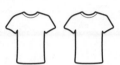

$\frac{1}{4}$ shaded　　$\frac{3}{4}$ unshaded

B

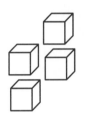　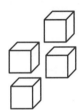　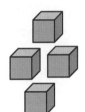　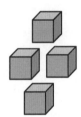

$\frac{2}{4}$ shaded　　$\frac{2}{4}$ unshaded

 Spot the mistake

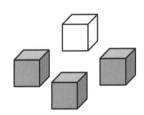　　$\frac{1}{3}$ of the cubes are shaded.

 Good to go?

What fraction of each set is shaded?

a)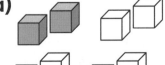
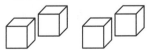

b)

c)

Understand that fractions join to make wholes

 Starting point

Tell the children that you made two sandwiches this morning. Explain that you cut each sandwich into equal parts. Ask:

- *How many equal parts might I have cut the sandwiches into?* Discuss that you might have cut them into two or four equal parts to make halves or quarters.
- *If I cut one sandwich into halves, how many halves do I have?* [2]
- *If I cut the other sandwich into quarters, how many quarters do I have?* [4]

Practical resources

- The 'Quarters cards' at the back of the book can be used to practise identifying missing fractions. Ask the children to pick a card and say what fraction of the item is missing or unshaded. Encourage them to give their answer in different ways, using halves and quarters.

Reveal graphic **A**. Point to the line of notation and ensure that the children understand that fractions can be joined together to make one whole. Then ask:

- *Could I join these parts of the sandwiches in different ways to make a whole sandwich, using some halves and some quarters?* Encourage the children to suggest making a whole from two-quarters and one-half.

Reveal graphic **B**. Ask a few further questions prompting the children to work out how many halves or quarters would make two wholes.

Give the children practical experience of combining halves and quarters using the idea in the **Practical resources** box.

> **Key point:** A whole can be made by combining fractional parts. One-half and two-quarters make one whole because two-quarters is equal to one-half.

 Spot the mistake

Ask:

- *The statement says '$\frac{3}{4} + \frac{1}{2} = 1$ whole'. Is this true?* [no]
- *Why isn't it true?* [If you joined the parts of the sandwiches together, you would have more than one sandwich.]
- *What do we need to do to make the statement true?* [Take away one-quarter of the sandwich. The statement would then read $\frac{3}{4} + \frac{1}{4} = 1$ whole or $\frac{2}{4} + \frac{1}{2} = 1$ whole.]

 Good to go?

Answers: a), d), e) and **f)**

Pupil book practice   Pages 8 and 9

In this unit the children practise combining halves and quarters and determine which combinations make wholes. Some of the questions are written in words and some are shown with fraction notation and symbols. There are also some questions that involve making more than one whole, for example from four halves or a collection of halves and quarters. In the **Challenge** section children will need to interpret the fraction notation and visualise the fractional parts to identify if wholes are made. Any children who struggle with this can be provided with plastic fraction equipment; for example, parts of circles can be joined together to see which make wholes.

➡️ Starting point

A

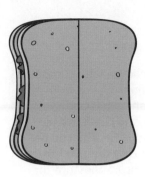   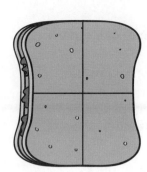

$\frac{1}{2} + \frac{1}{2} = 1$ whole $\frac{1}{4} + \frac{1}{4} + \frac{1}{4} + \frac{1}{4} = 1$ whole

B

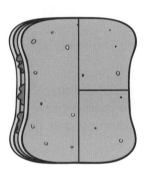 $\frac{1}{2} + \frac{2}{4} = 1$ whole

🔍 Spot the mistake

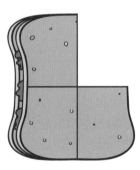 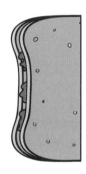 $\frac{3}{4} + \frac{1}{2} = 1$ whole

✔️ Good to go?

Which of these equal one whole?

a) four-quarters

b) three-halves

c) one-half plus one-quarter

d) $\frac{3}{4} + \frac{1}{4}$

e) $\frac{2}{4} + \frac{1}{2}$

f) $\frac{2}{4} + \frac{2}{4}$

Find $\frac{1}{2}$ of numbers and write fraction statements

➡ **Starting point**

Show graphic **A**, without the column of statements on the right. Ask:

● *What is half of 2? How can we find out?* Remind the children that, in order to find half, the whole set is split into two equal groups. Reveal the statement for this question showing the answer. [1]

Repeat the task for the other rows of ducks, finding half of each and then revealing the answer column. Draw attention to how the statements are written using notation, for example $\frac{1}{2}$ of 2 = 1.

Practical resources

● Provide the children with cubes. Ask them to make a stick from four, six or eight cubes and then to find how many cubes are in half of the stick. The stick can be broken in half and the two halves compared to ensure they are the same length.

Discuss any patterns the children can see in the questions and answers. The link between halving and doubling could also be made here. For example, if half of 6 is 3 then double 3 is 6.

Display graphic **B**. Now ask:

● *What numbers could we put in the empty boxes?* If the children suggest questions involving odd numbers, for example $\frac{1}{2}$ of 3, point out that 3 cannot be equally shared into two groups without cutting one of the items in half. For example, to share 3 apples equally into two groups, one of them would need to be cut in half. Children usually understand this concept quite easily when set in a food situation!

Give the children practical experience of finding halves using the idea in the **Practical resources** box.

> **Key point:** Half of a number of objects can be found by sorting the objects into two equal groups. This can be recorded using the notation $\frac{1}{2}$ of ☐ = ☐ .

🔍 **Spot the mistake**

Ask:

● *The statement says '$\frac{1}{2}$ of 10 = 20'. Is this true?* [no]

● *How could the statement be changed to make it true?* [The statement would be true if the numbers were in the order $\frac{1}{2}$ of 20 = 10. Alternatively, the statement could be changed to read $\frac{1}{2}$ of 10 = 5.]

✔ **Good to go?**

Answers: a) 6   **b)** 8   **c)** 10

Pupil book practice   Pages 10 and 11

This unit extends the idea of halving sets of objects. It provides increasingly complex problems to help the children begin to consolidate and generalise the concept of halving numbers rather than sets of objects. Encourage the children to look for patterns as they answer the questions.

Starting point

A What is $\frac{1}{2}$ of …?

$\frac{1}{2}$ of 2 = 1

$\frac{1}{2}$ of 4 = 2

$\frac{1}{2}$ of 6 = 3

$\frac{1}{2}$ of 8 = 4

B $\frac{1}{2}$ of ☐ = ☐

 Spot the mistake

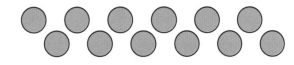 $\frac{1}{2}$ of 10 = 20

 Good to go?

a) Find $\frac{1}{2}$ of 12.

b) Find $\frac{1}{2}$ of 16.

c) Find $\frac{1}{2}$ of 20.

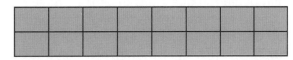

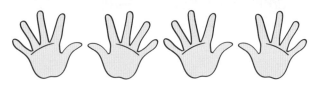

Make $\frac{1}{2}$, $\frac{1}{4}$ and $\frac{3}{4}$ turns and know $\frac{1}{2}$ is the same as $\frac{2}{4}$

➡ Starting point

Show graphic **A**. Ask:

- *What do the pictures show?* [a hand turning a dial] Help the children to understand that the first dial shows a full turn and the second shows a half turn. Draw attention to the white marker on each dial to indicate how far the dial has been turned.

Now reveal the quarter turns in graphic **B**. Ask:

- *How far has each dial been turned?* [one-quarter, two-quarter and three-quarter turns] Help the children to see each clockwise turn by following the arrow around, again drawing attention to the white marker that indicates how far the dial has been turned.

- *What do you notice about the half turn and the two-quarters turn?* [They are the same.]

Give the children practical experience of turns using the ideas in the **Practical resources** box.
For now, focus only on clockwise turns (from the children's perspective) so that the emphasis is on the size of the turns.

> **Practical resources**
>
> - Use equipment to show full, half and quarter turns, such as hands on a clock face, a wheel, a toy windmill or two plastic lengths joined to make an angle. Show that a half turn and a two-quarters turn are equal.
>
> - Square pictures, such as greetings cards, tiles or similar objects, can be turned to help children begin to visualise turns about the centre of an object.
>
> - Further turning work can be done by the children themselves. Ask them to face the board and then to turn clockwise through different turns.

> **Key point:** A full turn is when something is turned all the way round until it is in the same position again. Things can also be turned a fraction of a turn, such as a quarter turn, a half turn or a three-quarter turn. A half turn and a two-quarter turn are equal.

Spot the mistake

Ask:

- *Is the correct picture ticked?* [no]
- *Which of the pictures shows the boy after half a turn?* [the last one]
- *What turn is shown by the picture that is ticked?* [one-quarter turn (clockwise)]

Good to go?

Answers: a) 2   **b)** 1   **c)** 3

> ## Pupil book practice   Pages 12 and 13
>
> This unit provides the children with a range of turning questions set in different contexts. The children should only begin the questions after they have had considerable practical experience of turning things and themselves through half and quarter turns. The equivalence of one-half and two-quarters is explored (although the term 'equivalent' is not used until **Fractions 3**). The final question involves an anticlockwise turn which some children may find difficult without further support.

Starting point

A   a full turn $\frac{1}{2}$ turn

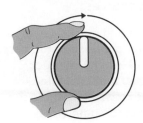   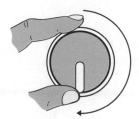

B $\frac{1}{4}$ turn $\frac{2}{4}$ turn $\frac{3}{4}$ turn

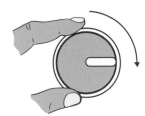   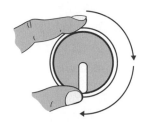   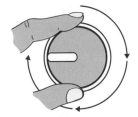

 Spot the mistake

   Tick the picture that shows the boy turned
through a $\frac{1}{2}$ turn.

☐   ☐   ✓   ☐

✔ **Good to go?**

What number will the dial point to after a:

a) $\frac{1}{2}$ turn?   **b)** $\frac{1}{4}$ turn?   **c)** $\frac{3}{4}$ turn?

Count in fractions and use $\frac{1}{2}$ and $\frac{2}{4}$ on number lines

➡ Starting point

Explain that you are going to count on in halves from 0. Display the stars in graphic **A**. Ask:

- *Can you see that each picture has half a star more than the one before it?* Point to each set of stars and ask the children to identify how many there are. [$\frac{1}{2}$, 1, $1\frac{1}{2}$, 2, $2\frac{1}{2}$, 3]

- Reveal the number line and notation. Ask the children to chant each number as you point to it in order. Continue the sequence beyond 3. Help them to notice that every other number is a whole number as two halves make a whole.

Reveal the top line of doughnuts in graphic **B**.
Explain that each picture has one-quarter more than the previous picture. Ask:

- *Can you count in quarters in a similar way?* Point to the pictures in order for the children to identify how many there are. [$\frac{1}{4}$, $\frac{2}{4}$, $\frac{3}{4}$, 1, $1\frac{1}{4}$, $1\frac{2}{4}$, $1\frac{3}{4}$, 2]

Reveal the number line and notation. Ask the children to chant the sequence and continue past 2. Discuss that every fourth number is a whole number as four-quarters make a whole.

Reveal the doughnuts and notation for $\frac{1}{2}$ and $1\frac{1}{2}$. Ask:

- *What do you notice about one-half and two-quarters of the doughnuts?* [They are equal.] Explain that either can be used when counting in quarters. Invite the children to count on in quarters again, but to use one-half rather than two-quarters in the sequence.

It is important that the children understand that the pattern of counting on in halves and quarters goes beyond 1, but there is no need yet to introduce the term 'mixed number'. Use the number lines as stated in the **Practical resources** box to support this work.

> **Key point:** When counting on in halves and quarters, numbers can be shown on a number line. $\frac{1}{2}$ and $\frac{2}{4}$ are equal and are therefore interchangeable on a number line.

🔍 Spot the mistake

Ask:

- *The sequence should be counting on in quarters. Can you spot the mistake in the sequence?* [$1\frac{1}{2}$ or $1\frac{2}{4}$ is missing.]

- *Can you count on in quarters correcting the mistake?*

✔ Good to go?

Answers: **a)** $\frac{1}{2}$　　**b)** $1\frac{1}{4}$　　**c)** $1\frac{3}{4}$　　**d)** $6\frac{1}{2}$ or $6\frac{2}{4}$

Pupil book practice　　　　　　　　　　　　　　　　Pages 14 and 15

Ensure children who find this work difficult have number lines to support them. As the children grow more confident in counting on in halves and quarters, they can begin to identify how many quarters are in several wholes, for example, 12 quarters in 3 wholes. In question 15 they are introduced to the idea that seven halves can be written as $3\frac{1}{2}$. This underpins later work (covered in **Fractions 3** onwards) in understanding the links between improper fractions and mixed numbers.

→ Starting point

A

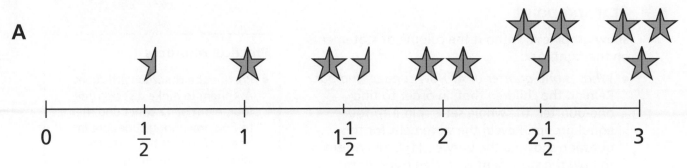

B

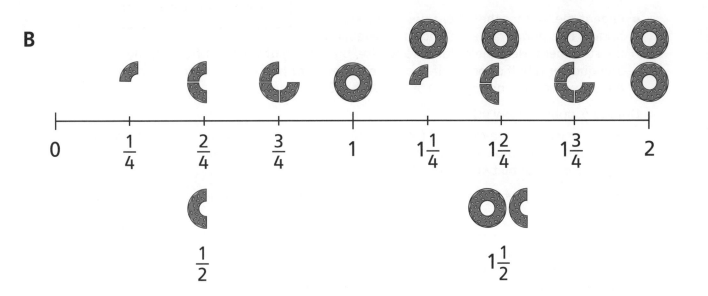

🔍 Spot the mistake

Count on in quarters.

$\frac{1}{4}$, $\frac{1}{2}$, $\frac{3}{4}$, 1, $1\frac{1}{4}$, $1\frac{3}{4}$, 2, $2\frac{1}{4}$, $2\frac{1}{2}$, $2\frac{3}{4}$, 3 ...

✔ Good to go?

What is the arrow pointing to?

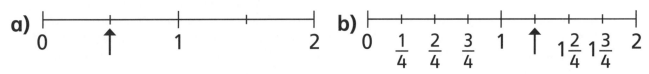

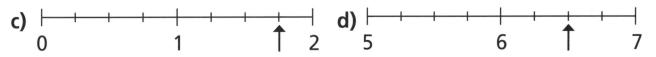

Find $\frac{1}{4}$ of numbers and write fraction statements

➡️ **Starting point**

Show graphic **A**, without the column of statements on the right. Ask:

- *What is one-quarter of 4? How can we find out?* Remind the children that, in order to find one-quarter, the whole set is split into four equal groups. Reveal the statement for this question showing the answer. [1] Draw attention to how the statement is written using notation: $\frac{1}{4}$ of 4 = 1.

- Repeat the task for the other rows of chicks, finding one-quarter of each and then revealing the statement. Help the children to realise, by looking at the sets of chicks, that one-quarter is half of one-half. So, if they know that half of 12 is 6, they can halve the answer to find one-quarter of 12 which is 3.

> **Practical resources**
>
> - Provide the children with cubes. Ask them to make a stick from four, eight or 12 cubes and then to find how many cubes are in one-half of half the stick. The stick can be broken into quarters and the parts compared to ensure they are the same length.

Display graphic **B**. Now ask:

- *How can we find one-quarter of 20?* Encourage the children to find different ways to solve this, for example using knowledge of half of 20, or by sorting 20 objects into four equal groups, or by two children holding up all their fingers.

Give the children practical experience of finding quarters using the idea in the **Practical resources** box.

> **Key point:** One-quarter of a number of objects can be found by sorting the objects into four equal groups. This can be recorded using the notation $\frac{1}{4}$ of ☐ = ☐ . One-quarter of a number can also be found by halving one-half of the number.

 Spot the mistake

Ask:

- *The statement says '$\frac{1}{4}$ of 40 = 20'. Is this true?* [no]
- *How could the statement be changed to make it true?* [$\frac{1}{2}$ of 40 = 20 or $\frac{1}{4}$ of 40 = 10]

 Good to go?

Answers: a) 8   **b)** 4   **c)** 12   **d)** 6

> ## Pupil book practice   Pages 18 and 19
>
> This unit extends the idea of finding quarters of sets of objects towards the more abstract notion of finding quarters of numbers. Some children may still need to use practical resources to help find the answers, while others may be more confident in working out answers numerically in their heads. Encourage the children to find one-half of a number first and then to use the answer to help them find one-quarter mentally (by halving). The **Challenge** questions involve larger numbers and, therefore, may not be suitable for the children who are still using practical equipment to find quarters.

Starting point

A What is $\frac{1}{4}$ of …?

4          $\frac{1}{4}$ of 4 = 1

8          $\frac{1}{4}$ of 8 = 2

12          $\frac{1}{4}$ of 12 = 3

B Find $\frac{1}{4}$ of 20.

Spot the mistake

  $\frac{1}{4}$ of 40 = 20

✔ **Good to go?**

a) Find $\frac{1}{2}$ of 16.   **b)** Find $\frac{1}{4}$ of 16.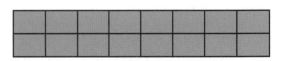

c) Find $\frac{1}{2}$ of 24.   **d)** Find $\frac{1}{4}$ of 24.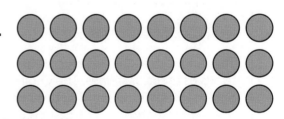

Understand the word 'third' and use the notation '$\frac{1}{3}$'

➡️ **Starting point**

Show the picture in graphic **A**. Ask:

- *How many equal slices has this Swiss roll been cut into?* [4]
- *What fraction of the Swiss roll is one slice?* [one-quarter]

Reveal the text to revise that one out of four equal parts is called one-quarter and is written as $\frac{1}{4}$.

Show the picture in graphic **B**. Ask:

- *How many equal slices has this Swiss roll been cut into?* [3]
- *One slice of this cake is one out of three equal slices. What is this fraction called?* [one-third] As the children may not be familiar with this term, explain that it means a whole has been split into three equal parts and ask them to say 'one out of three equal parts' and 'one-third' aloud.
- *Does anyone know, or can anyone guess, how to write one-third as a fraction, given that it is one out of three equal parts?* [$\frac{1}{3}$]

Reveal the text. Draw attention to the fact that the number on the bottom of the fraction shows how many equal parts the whole is split into while the number on the top shows how many of these parts are being described.

Use some of the ideas in the **Practical resources** box to reinforce the children's understanding of thirds and the relevant notation.

> **Practical resources**
>
> - Use objects that can be cut or folded into thirds, such as string, modelling clay, paper shapes or greetings cards.
> - Use objects where three identical pieces can be joined to make a whole, such as plastic shapes or collections of cubes.
> - The 'Thirds cards' at the back of the book can be used for matching activities. The cards can also be used with sets of real objects.

> **Key point:** The word 'third' is used when something is split into three equal parts. One-third is one out of three equal parts. It is written as $\frac{1}{3}$.

🔍 **Spot the mistake**

Ask:

- *The statement says '$\frac{1}{2}$ is shaded'. Is this true?* [no]
- *What is the mistake?* [One out of three equal parts is shaded, not one out of two.]
- *What fraction is shaded?* [one-third]
- *How do we write one-third?* [$\frac{1}{3}$]

✔️ **Good to go?**

Answers: Only **c)** is one-third shaded.

Explain that the three parts of **d)** must be equal for them to be thirds.

> **Pupil book practice**   **Pages 20 and 21**
>
> The questions in the **Get started** and **Now try these** sections are predominantly about thirds as areas of shapes. The **Challenge** section includes questions about thirds of sets of objects, of quantities, of full turns and of lengths. Observe which children struggle with these representations of fractions and provide them with more practice of these ideas using practical resources, such as cubes, hands on a clock face and string.

Starting point

A

one out of **four** equal parts

one-quarter $\frac{1}{4}$

B

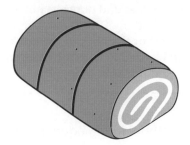

one out of **three** equal parts

one-third $\frac{1}{3}$

 Spot the mistake

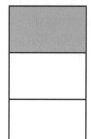 $\frac{1}{2}$ is shaded.

 Good to go?

Which of these shapes are one-third shaded?

a) 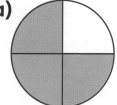   b) 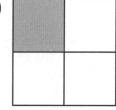   c)    d)

Find $\frac{1}{2}$, $\frac{1}{4}$ and $\frac{1}{3}$ of shapes, sets and lengths

➡ Starting point

This unit draws together all the fractions that have been introduced so far and shows mixed representations of these fractions. The aim is for the children to begin to generalise about how fractions work and to appreciate how the notation shows the equal parts of a whole.

Show the graphic without the notation beneath. Ask the children to imagine that each tube is a whole tube of sweets. Point to the second tube. Ask:

- *How many equal parts has this been split into?* [2]
- *What do we call each part?* [one-half]
- *How many halves make one whole?* [2]

Repeat for the tubes showing thirds and quarters. Once the children seem confident in their understanding of how the tubes are split, reveal the fractions beneath and ask the children to point to each fraction on one of the tubes. Each time ask:

- *What does the number on the bottom of a fraction show us?* [how many equal parts the whole is split into]
- *What does the number on the top show us?* [how many of these equal parts are being described]

Give the children practical experience of finding fractions using the ideas in the **Practical resources** box.

> **Practical resources**
>
> - Use objects that can be cut or divided into equal parts, such as paper plates, square or rectangular greetings cards, or modelling clay, to help the children practise finding fractions of shapes.
> - The 'Quarters of sets cards' and 'Thirds of sets cards' at the back of the book can be used to practise finding fractions of sets.
> - The 'Halves and quarters number lines' and the 'Thirds number line' posters at the back of the book can be used to help the children to find fractions of lengths.

> **Key point:** A whole can be split into equal parts to make halves (two equal parts), quarters (four equal parts) and thirds (three equal parts). The number on the bottom of the fraction shows how many equal parts the whole is split into. The number on the top shows how many of those parts are being described.

🗨 Spot the mistake

Ask:

- *The statement says that the picture shows three-quarters of the cake. Is this true?* [no]
- *What fraction of the cake does it show?* [one-third] *How do we write this as a fraction?* [$\frac{1}{3}$]

✔ Good to go?

Answers: a) $\frac{3}{4}$ **b)** $\frac{1}{4}$ **c)** $\frac{1}{2}$ or $\frac{2}{4}$ **d)** $\frac{1}{3}$

Pupil book practice   Pages 22 and 23

The pupil book provides practice in using notation for halves, quarters and thirds, including a range of different representations. Some questions in the **Challenge** section require the children to visualise fractions, without supporting artwork. If any children struggle with this, encourage them to draw pictures or use equipment to support their thinking.

Starting point

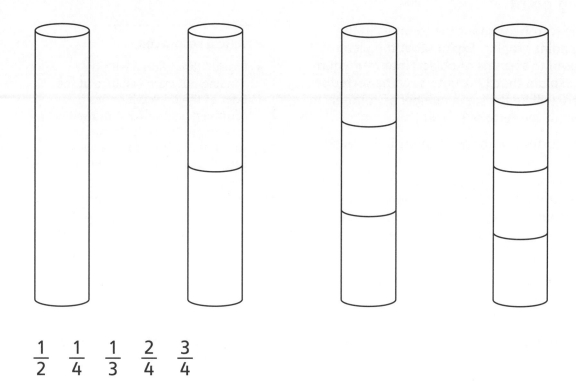

$\dfrac{1}{2}$ $\dfrac{1}{4}$ $\dfrac{1}{3}$ $\dfrac{2}{4}$ $\dfrac{3}{4}$

 Spot the mistake

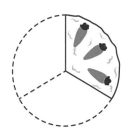   This shows $\dfrac{3}{4}$ of a cake.

 Good to go?

Which fraction goes with each picture?

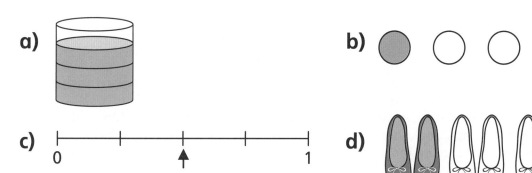

a)

b)

c)

d)

Find $\frac{1}{4}$, $\frac{2}{4}$ and $\frac{3}{4}$ of numbers

 Starting point

Show the tortoise without the counters in the **Starting point** graphic. Explain that the picture can be used to sort sets of objects into four equal groups. Explain that 12 counters can be sorted so that there will be the same number of counters in each part of the tortoise's shell.

> **Practical resources**
>
> ● Provide the children with the 'Finding quarters' resource at the back of the book which has a tortoise diagram like that used in this lesson. The children can use this to sort sets of objects, such as counters or cubes, into four equal groups.

Show the tortoise with the counters on its back. Ask:

● *How can we use this picture to tell us the answer to one-quarter of 12?* [The 12 counters are divided equally between the 4 parts of the shell, which shows us that the answer is 3.] Revise that when objects are in four equal groups the number in one group is one-quarter.

Show the questions under the tortoises. Ask:

● *What are the answers to these questions?* [$\frac{1}{4}$ of 12 = 3, $\frac{2}{4}$ of 12 = 6, $\frac{3}{4}$ of 12 = 9] Point out that once you know one-quarter of a number, two-quarters can be found by multiplying by 2 (or doubling) and three-quarters can be found by multiplying by 3.

Remind the children that four-quarters is the whole number of objects ($\frac{4}{4}$ of 12 = 12). Also discuss that two-quarters of a number is the same as one-half of the number, which might be quicker to solve.

Give the children practical experience of sorting sets using the idea in the **Practical resources** box.

> **Key point:** A quarter of a number of objects can be found by sorting them into four equal groups. Once one-quarter of a number is known, two-quarters can be found by multiplying by 2 (or doubling) and three-quarters can be found by multiplying by 3.

 Spot the mistake

Ask:

● *The statement says '$\frac{3}{4}$ of 16 = 4'. Is this true?* [no]
● *What is the mistake?* [$\frac{1}{4}$ not $\frac{3}{4}$ of 16 is 4.]
● *How can we find the correct answer?* [$\frac{3}{4}$ of 16 is found by multiplying 4 by 3 to give the correct answer 12.]

✔ **Good to go?**

Answers: a) 2　　**b)** 4　　**c)** 6　　**d)** 5　　**e)** 10　　**f)** 15

Pupil book practice　　　　　　　　　　　　　　　　　　**Pages 24 and 25**

This unit extends the idea of finding quarters of sets of objects towards the more abstract notion of finding quarters of numbers. Some children may still need to use practical resources to help them find the answers, while others may be more confident in working out answers numerically in their heads. Encourage the children to find one-quarter of a number first and then to use the answer to help them find two- and three-quarters mentally. The **Challenge** questions involve larger numbers and, therefore, may not be suitable for the children who are still using practical equipment to find quarters.

Starting point

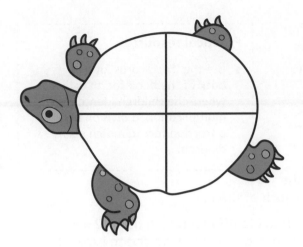   

$\frac{1}{4}$ of 12 = $\frac{2}{4}$ of 12 = $\frac{3}{4}$ of 12 =

🔍 **Spot the mistake**

 $\frac{3}{4}$ of 16 = 4

✔️ **Good to go?**

a) Find $\frac{1}{4}$ of 8.   **b)** Find $\frac{2}{4}$ of 8.   **c)** Find $\frac{3}{4}$ of 8.

⚪⚪ ⚪⚪   ⚪⚪ ⚪⚪

d) Find $\frac{1}{4}$ of 20.   **e)** Find $\frac{2}{4}$ of 20.   **f)** Find $\frac{3}{4}$ of 20.

⚪⚪⚪⚪⚪   ⚪⚪⚪⚪⚪   ⚪⚪⚪⚪⚪   ⚪⚪⚪⚪⚪

Connect fractions to multiplication and division facts

➡️ **Starting point**

Revise finding one-half, one-third and one-quarter by splitting or sharing into equal parts or groups.

Show the first set of cubes, without the text and notation, in the **Starting point** graphic. Ask:

- *This set of cubes is split into two equal groups. Can you give me a number fact for this set? It can be a multiplication fact, a division fact or a fraction fact.* [Prompt the children to identify $2 \times 4 = 8$, $8 \div 2 = 4$ and $\frac{1}{2}$ of $8 = 4$.] Reveal the list of facts and draw attention to the numbers in each of them.

> **Practical resources**
>
> - Use the 'Facts cards' at the back of the book for an activity where the children identify a multiplication, a division and a fraction fact to match each diagram.

Reveal the second set of cubes and repeat the task to identify facts such as $3 \times 2 = 6$, $6 \div 3 = 2$ and $\frac{1}{3}$ of $6 = 2$. Encourage the children to look at the numbers and to explore how multiplication and division facts are related to fraction facts.

Reveal the third set of cubes and repeat the task.

Give the children practical experience of connecting fraction facts to multiplication and division facts using the idea in the **Practical resources** box.

> **Key point:** Understand that fraction facts are related to multiplication and division facts.

🔍 **Spot the mistake**

Ask:

- *The statement says '$24 \div 3 = 8$ so $\frac{1}{3}$ of $8 = 24$'. Is this true?* [no]
- *What is the mistake?* [The numbers in the fraction fact are the wrong way round.]
- *What is the correct fraction fact?* [$\frac{1}{3}$ of $24 = 8$]

✔️ **Good to go?**

Answers: a) 8   **b)** 7   **c)** 7   **d)** 11

> ## Pupil book practice   Pages 26 and 27
>
> The **Get started** section provides visual representations of sets with related multiplication facts and asks children to answer fraction questions using these facts. Help the children to see the links between them. The later questions become increasingly abstract and children are asked to give answers without visual support. Observe which children struggle with these concepts and provide them with more practical experiences such as using the 'Facts cards' at the back of this book for further practice in linking facts and sets.

Starting point

one-half

share into 2 equal groups

$2 \times 4 = 8$ $8 \div 2 = 4$ $\frac{1}{2}$ of $8 = 4$

one-third

share into 3 equal groups

$3 \times 2 = 6$ $6 \div 3 = 2$ $\frac{1}{3}$ of $6 = 2$

one-quarter

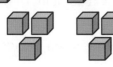

share into 4 equal groups

$4 \times 3 = 12$ $12 \div 4 = 3$ $\frac{1}{4}$ of $12 = 3$

Spot the mistake

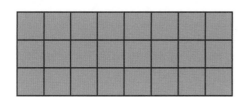

$24 \div 3 = 8$ so $\frac{1}{3}$ of $8 = 24$

Good to go?

Use the fact to find the answer.

a) $2 \times 8 = 16$

so $\frac{1}{2}$ of $16 =$

b) $3 \times 7 = 21$

so $\frac{1}{3}$ of $21 =$

c) $28 \div 4 = 7$

so $\frac{1}{4}$ of $28 =$

d) $33 \div 3 = 11$

so $\frac{1}{3}$ of $33 =$

Find fractions in a variety of representations

 Starting point

Show the **Starting point** graphic. Explain that it is important to know what the whole is when describing fractions. Wholes can take many forms including lengths, shapes, sets of objects, amounts of money, numbers, etc. Ask:

- *What is one-third of each of these wholes?* Go through each picture in turn and discuss how the whole has been split into three equal parts to show thirds and that one of these parts is one-third. Shade or mark one-third on the pictures. Explain that one-third of 60p is 20p and that one-third of 1 hour is 20 minutes.

- *Which of these fraction questions do you find easiest/hardest?* Discuss which representations the children find easiest or hardest to work with and remind them that, whatever the whole is, it is split into three equal parts as shown by the number on the bottom of the fraction. Provide additional examples of the representations that the children struggle with.

> **Practical resources**
>
> - Provide practical equipment to help with the representations that the children find most difficult. For example, for those who struggle with fractions on lines, provide them with the number lines at the back of this book. Encourage them to count on and back along the number lines to gain confidence.
> - The children can also practise the fractions by playing matching games with the photocopiable cards at the back of the book.

Give the children further experience of fractions in different representations using the ideas in the **Practical resources** box.

> **Key point:** Wholes can take many different forms. Whatever the whole, it is divided into equal parts as shown by the number on the bottom of the fraction.

 Spot the mistake

Ask:

- *The statement says that the point is marked one-third of the way along this line. Is the cross in the correct place on the line?* [no]
- *Where has the cross been drawn?* [halfway along]
- *Where should it be to show one-third?* [at the end of the first shaded section, one-third of the way along the line]

 Good to go?

Answers: a) $\frac{3}{4}$ **b)** $\frac{1}{2}$ **c)** $\frac{1}{3}$

> ## Pupil book practice   Pages 28 and 29
>
> The pupil book provides practice in using notation for halves, quarters and thirds, including a range of different representations. The **Challenge** section involves fraction questions that relate to measurements. If children struggle with this, encourage them to draw pictures or to use equipment to support their thinking.

Starting point

$\frac{1}{3}$ is one out of three equal parts of ...

| a whole shape | a whole set | a whole length | a whole turn |

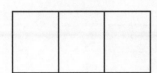 

| a whole line | a whole amount | a whole number | a whole hour |

$12 = 4 + 4 + 4$

Spot the mistake

The cross is $\frac{1}{3}$ of the way between A and B.

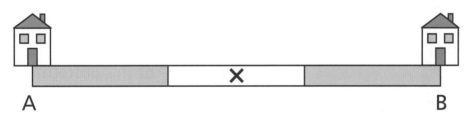

A   B

 Good to go?

a) What fraction of the whole shape is shaded?

b) What fraction of the whole set is unshaded?

c) What fraction of the whole line is marked?

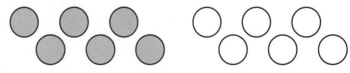

Know and use the notation for quarters of shapes

Key point

The word 'quarter' is used when something is split into **four equal parts**.
The number **4** on the **bottom** of a fraction tells us it is **quarters**.
The **top** number tells us **how many** quarters.

 $\frac{1}{4}$ $\frac{2}{4}$ $\frac{3}{4}$ $\frac{4}{4}$

one-quarter   two-quarters   three-quarters   four-quarters

Get started

1 Colour $\frac{1}{4}$ of the jigsaw.

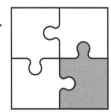

2 Tick the kite that is $\frac{3}{4}$ orange.

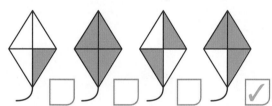

3 Complete the fraction to show two-quarters. $\frac{2}{4}$

4 Colour $\frac{2}{4}$ of the circle.

5 Write a fraction in the box to show how much of this flower is orange.

$\frac{3}{4}$

6 Colour $\frac{4}{4}$ of this pattern.

Now try these

7 Circle the fraction that shows three out of four equal parts.

$\frac{1}{4}$ $\frac{4}{3}$ $\frac{2}{4}$ $\left(\frac{3}{4}\right)$ $\frac{1}{2}$

8 Tick the picture that shows $\frac{3}{4}$ of a pie.

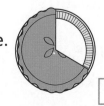   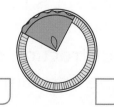   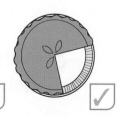

9 Circle the fraction that shows two-quarters.

$\frac{1}{4}$ $\left(\frac{2}{4}\right)$ $\frac{4}{4}$ $\frac{3}{4}$

10 Tick the squares that are $\frac{3}{4}$ shaded.

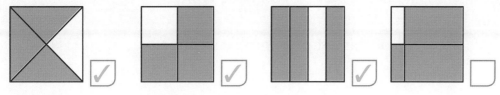

11 Circle the amount which is more:

$\frac{2}{4}$ of an apple $\left(\frac{3}{4} \text{ of an apple}\right)$

12 What number is on the bottom of the fraction when you write three-quarters in digits? __4__

Challenge

13 Fill in the box to show one whole. $\dfrac{4}{4}$

14 Jo eats $\frac{1}{4}$ of this sandwich.
What fraction of the sandwich is not eaten? $\frac{3}{4}$

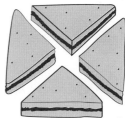

15 Two children each eat $\frac{1}{4}$ of a cereal bar. How much of the bar is left? $\frac{2}{4}$ or $\frac{1}{2}$

16 Yes or no? $\frac{1}{2}$ and $\frac{2}{4}$ are the same amount.

Yes ✓ No ☐

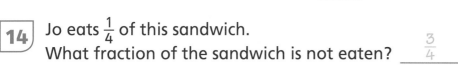

17 Yes or no? $\frac{3}{4}$ and $\frac{1}{4}$ together make a whole.

Yes ✓ No ☐

18 Write a fraction in the box to show the total of one-half of a cake and one-quarter of a cake.

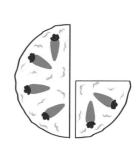

$\frac{1}{2} + \frac{1}{4} = \dfrac{3}{4}$

Know and use the notation for quarters of sets

Key point

To find **quarters** of a **set of objects**, sort the objects into **four equal groups**.

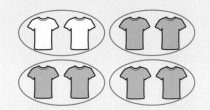

$\frac{1}{4}$ of this set of t-shirts is white.

$\frac{3}{4}$ of this set of t-shirts is orange.

Get started

1 What fraction of this set of cubes is orange? $\dfrac{1}{4}$

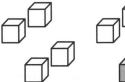

2 Colour one-quarter of this set of counters.

3 Draw crosses on three-quarters of the set of counters above.

4 These jelly beans are in 4 equal groups.

Draw a ring around $\frac{3}{4}$ of all the jelly beans.

5 Draw a ring around $\frac{3}{4}$ of this set of apricots.

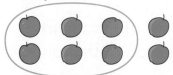

6 Yes or no? Two-quarters of these boots are stripy.

Yes ☑   No ☐

Now try these

7 Yes or no? $\frac{1}{4}$ of these counters are orange.   Yes ☐   No ☑

8 Tick the picture that does not show one-quarter of the rectangle shaded.

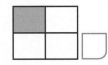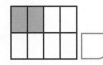☑

9   Which picture shows loops around two-quarters of the berries in the set?
Picture ___C___

Picture A   Picture B   Picture C

 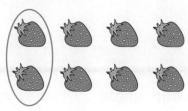 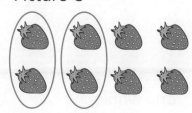

10   Here are 16 cakes.
How many cakes is $\frac{1}{4}$ of all the cakes? ___4___

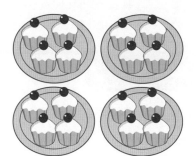

11   How many cakes is $\frac{2}{4}$ of all the cakes? ___8___

12   How many cakes is $\frac{3}{4}$ of all the cakes? ___12___

Challenge

13   A melon has 8 equal slices. How many slices is $\frac{2}{4}$ of the melon? ___4___

14   Becca has 8 grapes. How many grapes is $\frac{3}{4}$ of them? ___6___

15   There are 20 squares in the grid.
$\frac{1}{4}$ of the squares are orange.
Colour $\frac{2}{4}$ of the squares in a different colour.

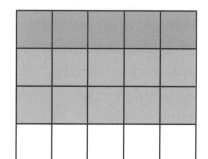

16   What fraction of the
20 squares are now not coloured? ___$\frac{1}{4}$___

17   A line is the same length as 12 cubes.
How many cubes are the same length as $\frac{3}{4}$ of the line? ___9___

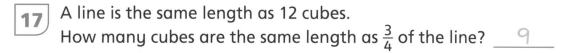

18   Complete the pattern.

$\frac{1}{4}$ of 12 is 3 $\frac{2}{4}$ of 12 is [6] $\frac{3}{4}$ of 12 is [9]

Understand that fractions join to make wholes

Key point

Two-halves make one whole.

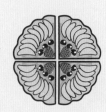

Four-quarters make one whole.

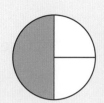

One-half and two-quarters make one whole.

One-quarter and three-quarters make one whole.

Get started

1 How many quarters make one whole? ___4___ quarters

2 Fill in the missing word.

One-half and one-___half___ together make one whole.

3 Draw dots on half of this circle and stripes on two-quarters. Is the whole circle patterned now?

Yes ☑ No ☐

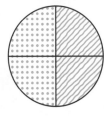

4 Yes or no? $\frac{1}{2} + \frac{1}{2} = 1$ whole

Yes ☑ No ☐

5 How many whole oranges are there in total?

___2___

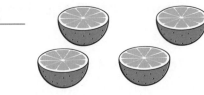

6 Yes or no? These pieces make one whole pizza in total.

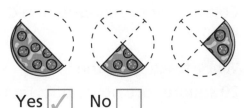

Yes ☑ No ☐

Now try these

7 Yes or no? One-half and two-quarters together make one whole. Yes ☑ No ☐

8 $\frac{1}{4}$ of a whole bun is eaten. What fraction of the bun is left? ___$\frac{3}{4}$___

9 Dan eats $\frac{1}{2}$ of a waffle and Sam eats $\frac{2}{4}$ of it. Is the whole waffle eaten? Yes ✓ No ☐

10 Kim eats $\frac{3}{4}$ of a biscuit. How much biscuit is left? ___$\frac{1}{4}$___

11 Yes or no? One-quarter and two-quarters together make one whole.

Yes ☐   No ✓

12 Fill in the missing word.

Two-quarters and two-__quarters__ together make one whole.

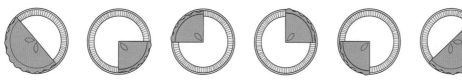

Challenge

13 How many whole pies are there in total? ___2___

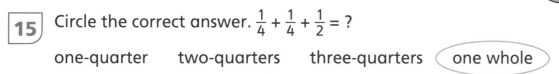

14 This glass is $\frac{2}{4}$ full of orange juice. Ben now fills the glass to the top. What fraction has he added? $\frac{2}{4}$ or $\frac{1}{2}$

15 Circle the correct answer. $\frac{1}{4} + \frac{1}{4} + \frac{1}{2} = ?$

one-quarter   two-quarters   three-quarters   (one whole)

16 How many wholes is this in total?

$\frac{1}{4} + \frac{1}{2} + \frac{1}{4} + \frac{1}{4} + \frac{1}{2} + \frac{1}{4} =$ ___2___

17 Jade spends one-quarter of her money on toys and half of her money on sweets. Circle the fraction of her money she has left. $\frac{1}{2}$ ($\frac{1}{4}$) $\frac{2}{4}$ $\frac{3}{4}$

18 Lou has three cans of cola. She drinks some cola out of each can. There is $\frac{1}{4}$ left in one can, $\frac{1}{2}$ left in another can and $\frac{3}{4}$ left in the last can. Is the total amount left more or less than a full can?

___more___

41

Find $\frac{1}{2}$ of numbers and write fraction statements

Key point

Half of a **number of objects** is found by sorting them into **two equal groups**.

Half of 8 ducks is 4 ducks.

Half of 8 is 4.

$\frac{1}{2}$ of 8 = 4

Get started

1 What number is half of 6? _____3_____

2 Colour half of this set of 8 hats.

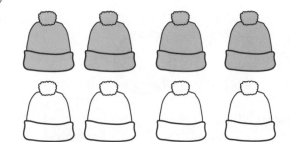

3 How many is $\frac{1}{2}$ of 8 hats? _____4_____

4 Fill in the missing number.

$\frac{1}{2}$ of 10 is | 5 |

5 Find $\frac{1}{2}$ of 4. _____2_____

6 Yes or no? $\frac{1}{2}$ of 2 is 1

Yes ✓   No ☐

Now try these

7 A farmer has 12 sheep. She puts half of them into a pen.

How many is that? _____6_____

8 One whole cake has 8 slices.

How many slices is half the cake? _____4_____

9 One-half of the 10 houses in this street are for sale.

How many houses are for sale? _____5_____

10 Halve the number 2.

_____1_____

11 A line is the same length as 12 cubes.

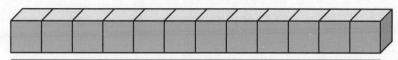

How many cubes are the same length as half the line?   __6__

12 Fill in the missing number. $\frac{1}{2}$ of [10] is 5

Challenge

13 It takes Ali 12 steps to walk from the door to his chair. How many steps does it take him to walk halfway from the door to his chair?   __6__

14 Fill in the missing numbers to show how many squares are orange.

$\frac{1}{2}$ of 6 is [3]

15 Fill in the missing numbers to show 'one-half of twenty equals ten'.

$\frac{1}{2}$ of [20] = [10]

16 A large pizza is cut into equal slices. One-half of the pizza is 6 slices. How many slices are in the whole pizza?   __12__

17 Complete the pattern.

$\frac{1}{2}$ of 2 = 1 $\frac{1}{2}$ of 4 = 2 $\frac{1}{2}$ of 6 = [3] $\frac{1}{2}$ of 8 = [4] $\frac{1}{2}$ of 10 = [5]

18 A factory makes 40 socks.
Halve 40 to find the number of pairs of socks it makes.   __20__

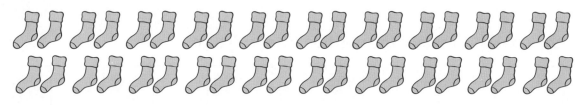

Make $\frac{1}{2}$, $\frac{1}{4}$ and $\frac{3}{4}$ turns and know $\frac{1}{2}$ is the same as $\frac{2}{4}$

Key point

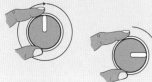

A **full turn** is when something is turned **all the way round** until it is in the same position again.

A $\frac{1}{4}$ turn is **one-quarter** of a full turn.

A $\frac{1}{2}$ turn or $\frac{2}{4}$ of a turn is **one-half** of a full turn.

A $\frac{3}{4}$ turn is **three-quarters** of a full turn.

Get started

1 This dial turns clockwise. What number will the line point to after half a turn from zero? _____2_____

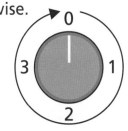

2 Look at the dial again. What number will the line point to after one-quarter of a turn from zero? _____1_____

3 Tim turns the dial clockwise from zero to the number 3. What fraction of a full turn is that?

$\frac{3}{4}$

4  This jigsaw piece is turned through a $\frac{1}{2}$ turn.

Tick to show what it looks like now.

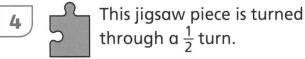

5 **A** Turn this tile a $\frac{1}{4}$ turn clockwise. Tick the correct answer.

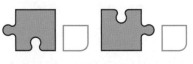

6 What object will this girl face after a $\frac{1}{2}$ turn?

the football

Now try these

7 This windmill has one orange sail. How many quarter turns are needed to bring the orange sail back to the same position? _____4_____

8 Tick the one which shows the position after a $\frac{1}{2}$ turn.

 →

9 What number will the big hand
on the clock point to after a $\frac{1}{4}$ turn?   _3_

10 The big hand of the clock points to 9 and
then turns clockwise to point to 6. How many
quarters of a full turn has the hand turned? $\frac{3}{4}$

11 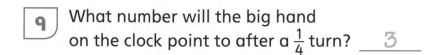 This tile is turned a $\frac{3}{4}$ turn clockwise. Tick to show what it looks like now.

☐   ☐   ☐   ✓

12 Yes or no? A turn of two-quarters is the same as half a turn. Yes ✓ No ☐

Challenge

13 Yes or no? If the top layer of this cube is turned a $\frac{1}{4}$ turn
clockwise, the orange squares will all be together.

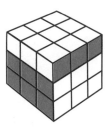

Yes ✓ No ☐

14 The big hand of a clock points to the number 4.
What number will it point to after a quarter turn clockwise?   _7_

15 Rose turns this lid clockwise. What turn has
Rose made? Write your answer as a fraction. $\frac{3}{4}$

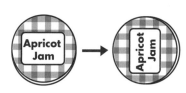

16 Lukas turns a $\frac{1}{4}$ turn clockwise. He then turns another $\frac{1}{4}$ turn clockwise.
Tick to show the total turn that Lukas has made.

$\frac{1}{4}$ turn ☐ $\frac{1}{2}$ turn ✓ $\frac{3}{4}$ turn ☐

17 Harry turns a key in a lock through half a turn. He then turns it a $\frac{1}{4}$ turn
more. What fraction of a whole turn has he turned the key altogether? $\frac{3}{4}$

18 Yes or no? If you turn a $\frac{1}{4}$ turn clockwise, you end up facing
the same way as if you had turned a $\frac{3}{4}$ turn anticlockwise.

Yes ✓ No ☐

Count in fractions and use $\frac{1}{2}$ and $\frac{2}{4}$ on number lines

Key point

Counting in **halves**

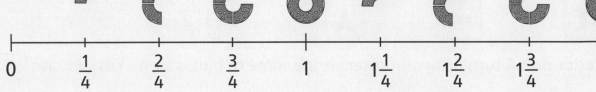

0	$\frac{1}{2}$	1	$1\frac{1}{2}$	2	$2\frac{1}{2}$	3

Counting in **quarters**

0	$\frac{1}{4}$	$\frac{2}{4}$	$\frac{3}{4}$	1	$1\frac{1}{4}$	$1\frac{2}{4}$	$1\frac{3}{4}$	2

Remember that **two-quarters** is equal to **one-half**.  =

Get started

1 How many stars are there?

$3\frac{1}{2}$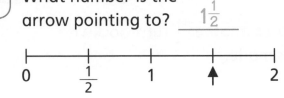

2 What number is one-half more than $1\frac{1}{2}$? $\underline{\quad 2 \quad}$

3 What number is the arrow pointing to? $1\frac{1}{2}$

0	$\frac{1}{2}$	1	2

4 How many doughnuts is this? $1\frac{1}{4}$

5 Write the missing fraction. $\frac{3}{4}$

0	$\frac{1}{4}$	$\frac{2}{4}$	↑	1	$1\frac{1}{4}$	$1\frac{2}{4}$	$1\frac{3}{4}$	2

6 Write the number of biscuits.

$3\frac{3}{4}$

Now try these

7 What is one-quarter more than $1\frac{3}{4}$? $\underline{\quad 2 \quad}$

8 When counting on in halves, what number comes between 3 and 4? $3\frac{1}{2}$

9 What is three-quarters more than $1\frac{1}{4}$? _____2_____

10 When counting on in quarters, what number comes between $2\frac{3}{4}$ and $3\frac{1}{4}$? _____3_____

11 How heavy are the apples?

_____$3\frac{1}{2}$_____ kg

12 What number is missing from the sequence?

0, $\frac{1}{2}$, 1, $1\frac{1}{2}$, 2, $2\frac{1}{2}$, _____3_____ , $3\frac{1}{2}$

Challenge

13 Write the next number in this sequence.

1, $1\frac{1}{4}$, $1\frac{1}{2}$, $1\frac{3}{4}$, 2, _____$2\frac{1}{4}$_____

14 Use the number line to help you find another way of writing a fraction equal to $\frac{1}{2}$. _____$\frac{2}{4}$_____

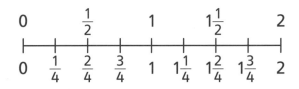

15 The length of Jamie's stride is half a metre. What is the length of 7 of Jamie's strides? _____$3\frac{1}{2}$_____ m

16 Yes or no? $2\frac{2}{4} = 2\frac{1}{2}$

Yes ✓   No ☐

17 A and B are marked on this line. Write their values.

A = _____$\frac{1}{4}$_____   B = _____$1\frac{3}{4}$_____

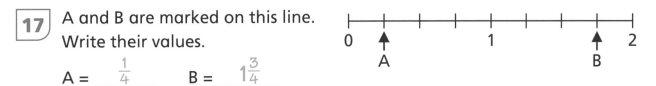

18 Count on six-quarters from zero. Fill in the boxes to show the answer in two different ways.

$1 \; \frac{2}{4}$ $1 \; \frac{1}{2}$

Check-up test 1

1 Tick the kite that is $\frac{1}{4}$ orange.

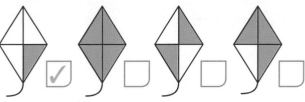

1 mark

2 Circle the fraction that shows three out of four equal parts.

$\left(\frac{3}{4}\right)$ $\quad \frac{2}{4}$ $\quad \frac{4}{3}$ $\quad \frac{1}{2}$ $\quad \frac{1}{4}$

1 mark

3 If Ella's family eats $\frac{3}{4}$ of this tart, how much is not eaten? $\quad \frac{1}{4}$

1 mark

4 What fraction of this set of cubes is white?

$\dfrac{3}{4}$

1 mark

5 Yes or no? $\frac{1}{4}$ of these counters are orange.

Yes ✓   No ☐

1 mark

6 A chocolate bar has 8 equal pieces. How many pieces are $\frac{2}{4}$ of the bar? $\quad 4$

1 mark

7 Yes or no? $\frac{1}{2} + \frac{1}{2} + \frac{1}{2} = 1$ whole

Yes ☐   No ✓

1 mark

8 Yes or no? Belle eats $\frac{2}{4}$ of a waffle and Dev eats $\frac{1}{2}$ of it. Is all of the waffle eaten?

Yes ✓   No ☐

1 mark

9 Tick the correct answer. $\frac{1}{4} + \frac{2}{4} = ?$

one-quarter ☐   two-quarters ☐   three-quarters ✓   one whole ☐

1 mark

10 What number is half of 8? _____ 4 _____

11 A farmer has 10 sheep.
He puts half of them into a barn.
How many is that? _____ 5 _____

1 mark

12 Fill in the missing numbers to show
'one-half of twelve equals six'.

$\dfrac{1}{2}$ of $\boxed{12}$ = $\boxed{6}$

1 mark

13  This jigsaw piece is turned clockwise through a $\frac{1}{4}$ turn.

Tick to show what it looks like now.

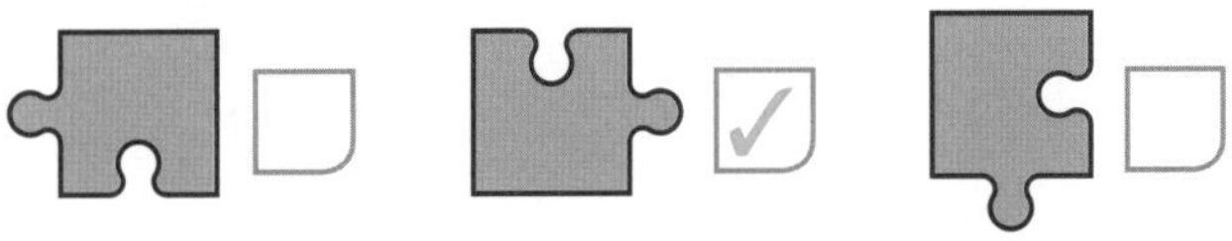

☐   ✓   ☐

1 mark

14 How many $\frac{1}{4}$ turns are in a full turn? _____ 4 _____

1 mark

15 Tom turns a key in a lock through a quarter turn.
He then turns it a half turn more.
What fraction of a whole turn
has he turned the key altogether? _____ $\frac{3}{4}$ _____

1 mark

16 What is one-quarter more than $1\frac{3}{4}$? _____ 2 _____

1 mark

17 When counting on in quarters, what
number comes between $1\frac{1}{4}$ and $1\frac{3}{4}$? _____ $1\frac{2}{4}$ _____ Also accept $1\frac{1}{2}$

1 mark

18 The length of Isha's stride is half a metre.
What is the length of 9 of Isha's strides? _____ $4\frac{1}{2}$ _____ m

1 mark

Total

18 marks

Find $\frac{1}{4}$ of numbers and write fraction statements

Key point

One-quarter of a **number of objects** is found by sorting them into **four equal groups**.

One-quarter of **12 chicks** is **3 chicks**.

$\frac{1}{4}$ of **12 = 3**

Get started

1 Colour $\frac{1}{4}$ of this set of 8 cubes.

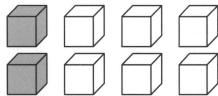

2 Now fill in the missing number.

$\frac{1}{4}$ of 8 is ⟨2⟩

3 One-quarter of these 4 squares are orange.

$\frac{1}{4}$ of 4 is ⟨1⟩

4 How many is one-quarter of 12 lollipops? ⟨3⟩

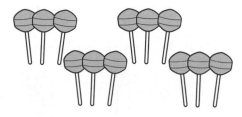

5 What is $\frac{1}{4}$ of 12? ⟨3⟩

6 Find one-quarter of 20. ⟨5⟩

Now try these

7 Here are 16 pieces of popcorn. How many is one-quarter of the whole set? ⟨4⟩

8 Write the missing number. $\frac{1}{4}$ of 16 is 4

9 Fill in the missing number.

$\frac{1}{4}$ of 12 ants is ⟨3⟩ ants.

10 One whole pie has 8 slices.

How many slices is one-quarter of the pie? ___2___

11 One-quarter of the 16 tiles are orange.
Fill in the missing numbers.

$\frac{1}{4}$ of 16 is | 4 |

12 Mia has 40p.

What is $\frac{1}{4}$ of 40p? ___10___ p

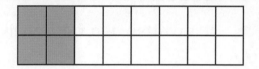

Challenge

13 When 24 sweets are shared equally between 4 children, each gets 6 sweets.
Write the numbers in the boxes below to make a true statement.

$\frac{1}{4}$ of | 24 | is | 6 |

14 A football club has 20 children. $\frac{1}{4}$ of them are boys.

How many are boys? ___5___

15 A farmer has 40 sheep. She puts $\frac{1}{4}$ of them into a field.

How many is that? ___10___

16 There are 60 minutes in 1 hour.

How many minutes are there in $\frac{1}{4}$ of an hour? ___15___ min

17 Complete the pattern.

$\frac{1}{4}$ of 20 = 5 $\frac{1}{4}$ of 40 = | 10 | $\frac{1}{4}$ of 60 = | 15 | $\frac{1}{4}$ of 80 = | 20 | $\frac{1}{4}$ of 100 = | 25 |

18 How many pence is $\frac{1}{4}$ of £1? ___25___ p

Understand the word 'third' and use the notation '$\frac{1}{3}$'

Key point

The word **'third'** is used when something is split into **three equal parts**.
Each part is **one-third** of the whole.

One-third is one out of three equal parts.

It is written as a fraction like this: $\frac{1}{3}$

Get started

1 Colour one-third of this circle.

2 Yes or no?
This is one-third of a pizza.

Yes ☐   No ☑

3 Yes or no? One-third of this shape is orange.
Yes ☐   No ☑

4 How many equal pieces should this cupcake be cut into to give thirds? __3__

5 Fill in the missing word.
A whole is split into three equal parts. Each part is called one-___third___.

6 Fill in the missing numbers.
$\frac{1}{3}$ of the whole glass is filled.

Now try these

7 A paper plate is cut into thirds.
How many thirds are there? __3__

8 What fraction of the starfish are orange? __$\frac{1}{3}$__

9 Tick the squares that are one-third shaded.

 ✓   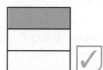 ✓   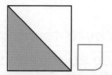 ☐   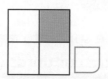 ☐   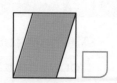 ☐

10 Two-thirds of a whole cake have been eaten.

Write a fraction to show how much of the cake has not been eaten. $\frac{1}{3}$

11 Which is larger? Circle it.

one-third   (one-half)

1	
$\frac{1}{2}$	$\frac{1}{2}$
$\frac{1}{3}$	$\frac{1}{3}$	$\frac{1}{3}$

12 Yes or no?

Three-thirds together make a whole.   Yes ✓   No ☐

Challenge

13 The big hand of a clock points to 12.

It then turns clockwise through one-third of a full turn.

What number does it point to now?   4

14 Draw a line in the box that is one-third of the length of this line.

15 How many counters are there in $\frac{1}{3}$ of this set?   2

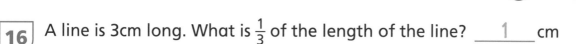

16 A line is 3cm long. What is $\frac{1}{3}$ of the length of the line?   1 cm

17 Yes or no? $\frac{1}{3} + \frac{1}{3} + \frac{1}{3} + \frac{1}{3} = 1$ whole   Yes ☐   No ✓

18 One whole is divided by 3 to give what fraction? $1 \div 3 = \frac{1}{3}$

Find $\frac{1}{2}$, $\frac{1}{4}$ and $\frac{1}{3}$ of shapes, sets and lengths

Key point

A **whole** can be split into equal parts to make **halves** (two equal parts), **quarters** (four equal parts) or **thirds** (three equal parts).

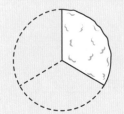

$$\frac{1}{3}$$

The number on the **bottom** of a fraction shows **how many equal parts** the **whole** is split into.

The number on the **top** of the fraction shows **how many of those parts** are being described.

Get started

1 Circle the fraction of this square that is orange.

$\frac{1}{4}$ $\frac{4}{4}$ $\left(\frac{1}{2}\right)$ $\frac{3}{4}$

2 Colour $\frac{1}{4}$ of the circle.

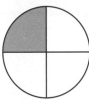

3 Fill in the box to show one-third. $\dfrac{1}{3}$

4 What fraction of this jar is filled?

$\dfrac{3}{4}$

5 A is marked on this line. What is its value? $A = \dfrac{1}{3}$

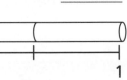

0   A   1

6 Draw a ring around half of these cakes.

Now try these

7 What fraction of these pencils are orange? $\dfrac{3}{4}$

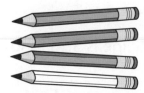

8 What fraction of these shoes are stripy? $\dfrac{1}{4}$

9 What number is the arrow pointing to? $\frac{3}{4}$

10 Mark a cross at the point $\frac{2}{4}$ of the way from house A to house B.

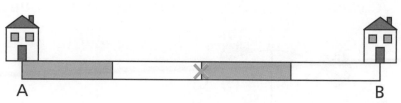

11 How many thirds make up two wholes? 6

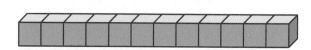

12 A line is the same length as 12 cubes. How many cubes are the same length as one-quarter of this line? 3

Challenge

13 Josh has 40p.

What is $\frac{3}{4}$ of 40p? 30 p

14 Colour $\frac{2}{4}$ of the squares in this grid.

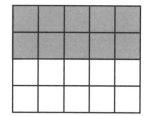

15 How many buttons are there in $\frac{3}{4}$ of this set? 6

16 What fraction of this whole packet is 2 biscuits? $\frac{1}{4}$

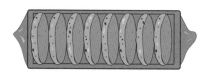

17 A line is 15cm long. What is $\frac{1}{3}$ of the length of the line? 5 cm

18 The number $1\frac{2}{4}$ is marked on a number line.

What number is $\frac{1}{2}$ more than this number? 2

Find $\frac{1}{4}$, $\frac{2}{4}$ and $\frac{3}{4}$ of numbers

Key point

A **whole set** can be sorted into **four equal groups** to show **quarters**.

One-quarter of **12** counters is **3** counters.

$\frac{1}{4}$ of **12** is **3**

Two-quarters of **12** counters is **6** counters.

$\frac{2}{4}$ of **12** is **6**

Three-quarters of **12** counters is **9** counters.

$\frac{3}{4}$ of **12** is **9**

Get started

1 Colour $\frac{3}{4}$ of this set of 4 cubes.

2 Now write the answer.

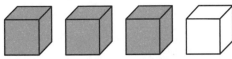

$\frac{3}{4}$ of 4 is $\boxed{3}$

3 Two-quarters of these 16 squares are orange.

$\frac{2}{4}$ of 16 is $\boxed{8}$

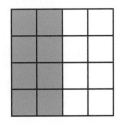

4 How many is three-quarters of 12 apricots?

___9___

5 What is $\frac{2}{4}$ of 8p?

___4___ p

6 Yes or no? $\frac{2}{4}$ is equal to $\frac{1}{2}$.

Yes ✓   No ☐

Now try these

7 Find two-quarters of 20. ___10___

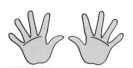

8 Here are 24 pieces of popcorn. How many is one-quarter of the whole set? ___6___

9 Fill in the missing number.

$\frac{3}{4}$ of 12 bees is [9] bees.

10 What is $\frac{2}{4}$ of 40p? ___20___ p

11 What is $\frac{2}{4}$ of 16? ___8___

12 There are 60 minutes in 1 hour.
How many minutes are
there in $\frac{3}{4}$ of an hour? ___45___ min

Challenge

13 Yes or no? One-quarter of a number can be found by dividing it by 4.

Yes [✓]   No [ ]

14 Complete the pattern.

$\frac{1}{4}$ of 24 = 6 $\frac{2}{4}$ of 24 = [12] $\frac{3}{4}$ of 24 = [18] $\frac{4}{4}$ of 24 = [24]

15 In this rectangle 12 out of the 16 squares are orange.
Write what fraction of the rectangle is orange.

[$\frac{3}{4}$] of 16 is 12

16 When 32 sweets are shared equally between
4 children, each gets 8 sweets. What is $\frac{2}{4}$ of 32 sweets? ___16___

17 A farmer has 32 chickens. He puts $\frac{3}{4}$ of them
into the hen house. How many chickens is that? ___24___

18 A hockey club has 100 children.
$\frac{3}{4}$ of them are boys. How many are boys? ___75___

Connect fractions to multiplication and division facts

Key point

To find **one-half** of a set, share into **two equal groups**.

　　$2 \times 4 = 8$　　$8 \div 2 = 4$　　$\frac{1}{2}$ of $8 = 4$

To find **one-third** of a set, share into **three equal groups**.

　　$3 \times 2 = 6$　　$6 \div 3 = 2$　　$\frac{1}{3}$ of $6 = 2$

To find **one-quarter** of a set, share into **four equal groups**.

$4 \times 2 = 8$　　$8 \div 4 = 2$　　$\frac{1}{4}$ of $8 = 2$

Get started

1 Two groups of 6 are 12, so what is $\frac{1}{2}$ of 12? ___6___

2 Three lots of 4 are 12, so what is $\frac{1}{3}$ of 12? ___4___

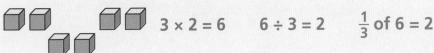

3 Four times 5 is 20, so what is $\frac{1}{4}$ of 20? ___5___

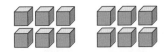

4 Three lots of 10p make 30p. What is $\frac{1}{3}$ of 30p?

___10___ p

5 This grid has 24 squares arranged in 3 rows of 8.

What is $\frac{1}{3}$ of 24? ___8___

6 This grid has 28 squares arranged in 4 rows of 7.

What is $\frac{1}{4}$ of 28? ___7___

Now try these

7 Divide 18 by 2 to find the answer to $\frac{1}{2}$ of 18. ___9___

8 | $3 \times 5p = 15p$ | Use this fact to find $\frac{1}{3}$ of 15p. ___5___ p

9 There are eighteen beanbags in three piles of six.

What is $\frac{1}{3}$ of 18 beanbags? ___6___

10 Li knows that 24 divided by 2 is 12.
Use this fact to give the answer to $\frac{1}{2}$ of 24cm. ___12___ cm

11 4 × 10 = 40, so what is $\frac{1}{4}$ of 40? ___10___

12 Find one-quarter of
the length of this line. ___4___ cm

```
1  2  3  4  5  6  7  8  9  10 11 12 13 14 15 16 17 18 19 20
cm
```

Challenge

13 One-quarter of a class of 16 children
wear glasses. How many wear glasses? ___4___

14 Alice spends one-third of £36 to buy a bag costing £12.
Fill in the missing numbers.

3 × £ $\boxed{12}$ = £36 $\frac{1}{3}$ of £36 is £12   £36 ÷ $\boxed{3}$ = £12

15 Find $\frac{1}{4}$ of 400g. ___100___ g

16 Tick the statements that are true.

If 4 × 8 = 32, then $\frac{1}{4}$ of 8g is 32g. ☐

If 3 × 11 = 33, then $\frac{1}{3}$ of 33cm is 11cm. ☑

If 38 ÷ 2 = 19, then $\frac{1}{2}$ of 38 is 19. ☑

17 Write three different true statements. *Also accept $\frac{1}{6}$ of 12 is 2, $\frac{1}{12}$ of 12 is 1*

$\frac{1}{2}$ of 12 is $\boxed{6}$ $\frac{1}{3}$ of 12 is $\boxed{4}$ $\frac{1}{4}$ of 12 is $\boxed{3}$

18 Find $\frac{1}{3}$ of £9 plus $\frac{1}{3}$ of £6. £___5___

Find fractions in a variety of representations

Key point

Wholes can take many forms. If you split **any whole** into equal parts, you get fractions like halves and quarters.

Here **different wholes** are all split into **three equal parts**. Each part is $\frac{1}{3}$ or **one-third** which is 'one out of three equal parts'.

a whole shape	a whole set	a whole length	a whole turn
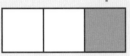		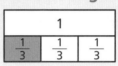	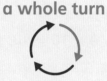
a whole line	a whole amount	a whole number	a whole hour
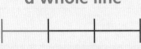		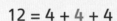 12 = 4 + 4 + 4	

Get started

1 Tick the shape that is $\frac{3}{4}$ orange.

   ✓

2 Draw a ring around $\frac{1}{4}$ of the caterpillars.

3 What fraction of the cubes are orange? $\frac{1}{3}$ or $\frac{4}{12}$

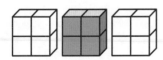

4 Mark $\frac{3}{4}$ on this line with a cross.

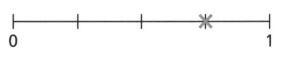

5 What fraction of this jar is filled? $\frac{2}{3}$

6 A line is 8 cubes long. How many cubes are the same length as one-quarter of this line? 2

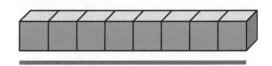

Now try these

7 ↑ An arrow points up.
Draw what it will look like after a $\frac{1}{2}$ turn.

8 What is $\frac{1}{2}$ of 16? ___8___

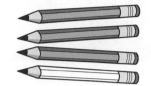

9 What fraction of these pencils are white? ___$\frac{1}{4}$___

10 Fill in the missing numbers in this sequence:

4, $4\frac{1}{4}$, $4\frac{1}{2}$, $4\frac{3}{4}$, ___5___, $5\frac{1}{4}$, $5\frac{1}{2}$, ___$5\frac{3}{4}$___, 6, ___$6\frac{1}{4}$___

11 What number is the arrow pointing to? ___$8\frac{3}{4}$___

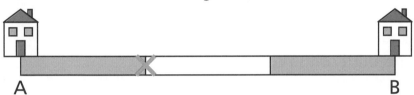

12 Mark a cross at the point $\frac{1}{3}$ of the way from house A to house B.

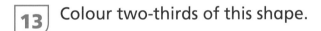

A   B

Challenge

13 Colour two-thirds of this shape.

14 What is $\frac{3}{4}$ of £8? £___6___

15 There are 60 minutes in an hour.
How many minutes are there in $1\frac{1}{2}$ hours? ___90___min

16 Sandeep wins some money. He gives $\frac{1}{3}$ of the money to his son and $\frac{1}{3}$ of the money to his daughter. He keeps the rest.
What fraction of the money does Sandeep keep? ___$\frac{1}{3}$___

17 $7\frac{2}{4}$ kg is marked on a number line.
What number is $1\frac{1}{2}$ kg more than this number? ___9___ kg

18 One-quarter of the biscuits in a packet are chocolate. Three biscuits are chocolate. How many biscuits are in the whole packet altogether? ___12___

Check-up test 2

1 What is $\frac{1}{4}$ of 8? ___2___

2 Here are 12 hats.
How many is
one-quarter of the set? ___3___

3 A dance class has 24 children.
$\frac{1}{4}$ of them are boys. How many are boys? ___6___

4 How many equal pieces should
this cake be cut into to give thirds? ___3___

5 Lucy and Finn have a whole cake. Lucy eats one-third
of the cake. Finn eats one-third of the cake. Write a
fraction to show how much of the cake is not eaten. ___$\frac{1}{3}$___

6 How many counters are
there in $\frac{1}{3}$ of this set? ___3___

7 Colour $\frac{3}{4}$ of the circle.

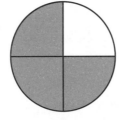

8 What fraction of
these buttons are white? ___$\frac{1}{4}$___

9 Colour $\frac{3}{4}$ of the 20 squares in this grid.

10 What is $\frac{2}{4}$ of 8p? ___4___ p

11   What is $\frac{1}{4}$ of 16?   _4_

                                                        1 mark

12   28 sweets are shared equally between 4 children. Each gets 7 sweets. What is $\frac{2}{4}$ of 28 sweets?   _14_

                                                        1 mark

13   This grid has 21 squares arranged in 3 rows of 7.

     What is $\frac{1}{3}$ of 21?   _7_

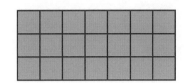

                                                        1 mark

14   Find one-third of the length of this line.   _5_   cm

                                                        1 mark

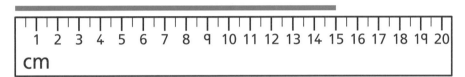

15   Find $\frac{1}{3}$ of £12 plus $\frac{1}{3}$ of £3.   £ _5_

                                                        1 mark

16   Draw a ring around $\frac{1}{4}$ of the coins.

                                                        1 mark

17   Mark a cross at the point $\frac{2}{3}$ of the way from house A to house B.

      A   B   1 mark

18   The number $5\frac{3}{4}$ is marked on a number line.

     What number is $\frac{1}{2}$ more than this number?   _$6\frac{1}{4}$_

                                                        1 mark

Total

18 marks

Final test

Section 1

1 How many equal parts is a whole split into to show quarters? ___4___   1 mark

2 Colour $\frac{1}{3}$ of this shape.    1 mark

3 Write a word to show what fraction of this flag is orange.

one-___third___ 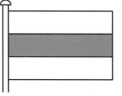   1 mark

4 What fraction of the jelly beans are orange? ___$\frac{1}{4}$___   1 mark

5 A line is 16 cubes long. How many cubes are the same length as one-quarter of this line? ___4___   1 mark

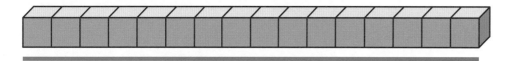

6 A line is 6cm long.
What is $\frac{1}{3}$ of the length of the line? ___2___ cm   1 mark

7 Circle the fraction that shows three out of four equal parts.

$\frac{1}{3}$ $\frac{4}{3}$ $\frac{2}{4}$ $\left(\frac{3}{4}\right)$ $\frac{1}{2}$ 1 mark

8 $\boxed{4 \times 10 = 40}$ Use this fact to find $\frac{1}{4}$ of 40m. ___10___ m   1 mark

9 Here are 16 cakes.
How many cakes is $\frac{2}{4}$ of them all? ___8___   1 mark

10 Tick the correct answer. $\frac{1}{4} + \frac{1}{2} = $?

one-quarter ☐   two-quarters ☐

three-quarters ☑   one whole ☐   1 mark

Section 2

11 Write three-quarters as a fraction. ___$\frac{3}{4}$___

1 mark

12 Fill in the missing number.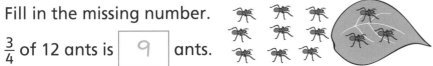

$\frac{1}{2}$ of 10 is [5]

1 mark

13 Divide 14 by 2 to find the answer to $\frac{1}{2}$ of 14kg. ___7___ kg

1 mark

14 Fill in the missing number.

$\frac{3}{4}$ of 12 ants is [9] ants.

1 mark

15 Yes or no? Two-quarters is the same as one-half.

Yes [✓]   No [ ]

1 mark

16 How many $\frac{1}{4}$ turns are in a half turn? ___2___

1 mark

17 Arun eats $\frac{1}{2}$ of a waffle and Milly eats $\frac{2}{4}$ of it. Is the whole waffle eaten?

Yes [✓]   No [ ]

1 mark

18 Complete the pattern.

$\frac{1}{4}$ of 24 is 6 $\frac{2}{4}$ of 24 is [12] $\frac{3}{4}$ of 24 is [18]

1 mark

19 Count on ten-quarters from zero. Fill in the boxes to show the answer in two different ways.

[$2\frac{2}{4}$]   [$2\frac{1}{2}$]

1 mark

20 $7\frac{2}{4}$kg is marked on a number line. What number is $1\frac{1}{2}$kg less than this number? ___6___ kg

1 mark

Total

[ ]

20 marks

End of test

Pupil progress chart

Pupil's name _____   Class / set _____

Unit	Get started		Now try these		Challenge		Total	
1		6		6		6		18
2		6		6		6		18
3		6		6		6		18
4		6		6		6		18
5		6		6		6		18
6		6		6		6		18
Check-up test 1								18
7		6		6		6		18
8		6		6		6		18
9		6		6		6		18
10		6		6		6		18
11		6		6		6		18
12		6		6		6		18
Check-up test 2								18

Final test group record sheet

Pupil's name		Y2/F1										Y2/F2										Total
	1	2	3	4	5	6	7	8	9	10	11	12	13	14	15	16	17	18	19	20	/20

Quarters cards

one-quarter	two-quarters	three-quarters
$\frac{1}{4}$	$\frac{2}{4}$	$\frac{3}{4}$

Quarters of sets cards

one-quarter	two-quarters	three-quarters
$\frac{1}{4}$	$\frac{2}{4}$	$\frac{3}{4}$

Thirds cards

one-third	not one-third	$\frac{1}{3}$	not $\frac{1}{3}$

Thirds of sets cards

one-third	not one-third	$\frac{1}{3}$	not $\frac{1}{3}$

 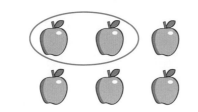 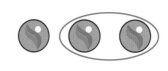
  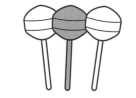
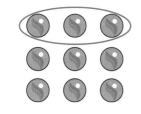  

 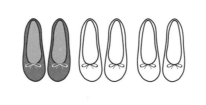 
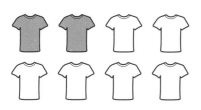  

Halves and quarters number lines

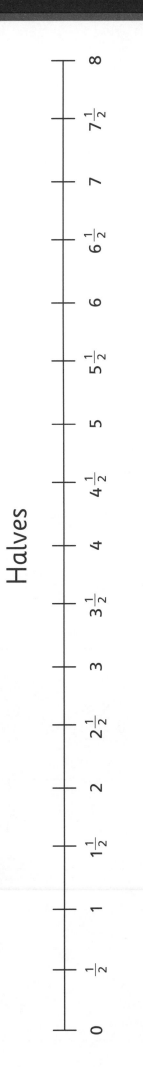

Halves

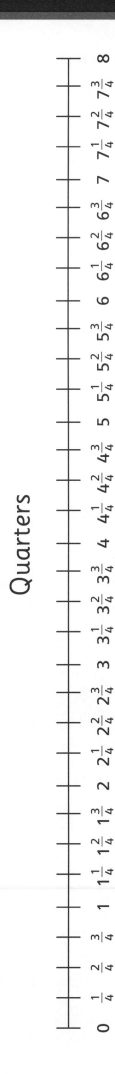

Quarters

Thirds number line

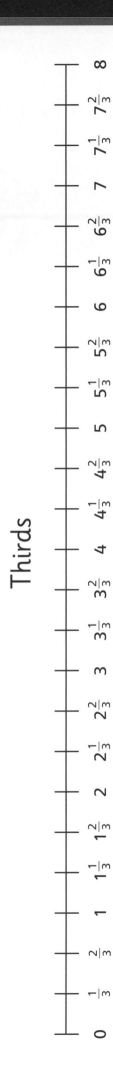

Thirds

0 $\frac{1}{3}$ $\frac{2}{3}$ 1 $1\frac{1}{3}$ $1\frac{2}{3}$ 2 $2\frac{1}{3}$ $2\frac{2}{3}$ 3 $3\frac{1}{3}$ $3\frac{2}{3}$ 4 $4\frac{1}{3}$ $4\frac{2}{3}$ 5 $5\frac{1}{3}$ $5\frac{2}{3}$ 6 $6\frac{1}{3}$ $6\frac{2}{3}$ 7 $7\frac{1}{3}$ $7\frac{2}{3}$ 8

Finding quarters

Sort sets into 4 equal groups to find quarters.

Facts cards

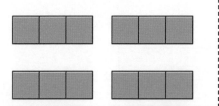 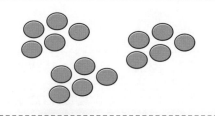 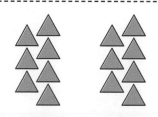

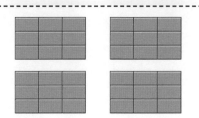 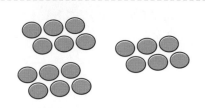 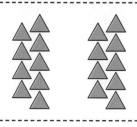

$\frac{1}{4}$ of 12 = 3	$\frac{1}{3}$ of 15 = 5	$\frac{1}{2}$ of 14 = 7
$\frac{1}{4}$ of 36 = 9	$\frac{1}{3}$ of 18 = 6	$\frac{1}{2}$ of 18 = 9
4 × 3 = 12	3 × 5 = 15	2 × 7 = 14
4 × 9 = 36	3 × 6 = 18	2 × 9 = 18
12 ÷ 4 = 3	15 ÷ 3 = 5	14 ÷ 2 = 7
36 ÷ 4 = 9	18 ÷ 3 = 6	18 ÷ 2 = 9

Full list of books in the Fractions, Decimals and Percentages series

Pupil books

Fractions 1	ISBN 978 0 7217 1375 5
Fractions 2	ISBN 978 0 7217 1377 9
Fractions 3	ISBN 978 0 7217 1379 3
Fractions 4	ISBN 978 0 7217 1381 6
Fractions 5	ISBN 978 0 7217 1383 0
Fractions 6	ISBN 978 0 7217 1385 4

Teacher's guides

Fractions 1 Teacher's Guide	ISBN 978 0 7217 1376 2
Fractions 2 Teacher's Guide	ISBN 978 0 7217 1378 6
Fractions 3 Teacher's Guide	ISBN 978 0 7217 1380 9
Fractions 4 Teacher's Guide	ISBN 978 0 7217 1382 3
Fractions 5 Teacher's Guide	ISBN 978 0 7217 1384 7
Fractions 6 Teacher's Guide	ISBN 978 0 7217 1386 1

Free downloads available from the Schofield & Sims website

A selection of free downloads is available from the Schofield & Sims website (www.schofieldandsims.co.uk/free-downloads). These may be used to further enhance the effectiveness of the programme. The downloads add to the range of print materials supplied in the teacher's guides.

- **Graphics** slides containing the visual elements from each teacher's guide unit provided as Microsoft PowerPoint® presentations.

- **Go deeper investigations** providing additional extension material to develop problem-solving and reasoning skills.

- **Additional resources** including a fraction wall, a comparison chart and number lines to support learning and teaching.